# Child Survivors and Perpetrators of Sexual Abuse

This book is dedicated to my Grandma, Pauline LaFollette, and the first Dr. Hunter, William Frank, for showing me that authors are everyday people and to Norma Hunter for ensuring that I had a childhood filled with books.

# Child Survivors and Perpetrators of Sexual Abuse

## Treatment Innovations

## Mic Hunter
### EDITOR

**SAGE** Publications
*International Educational and Professional Publisher*
Thousand Oaks   London   New Delhi

*For information address*:

 SAGE Publications, Inc.
2455 Teller Road
Thousand Oaks, California 91320

SAGE Publications Ltd.
6 Bonhill Street
London EC2A 4PU
United Kingdom

SAGE Publications India Pvt. Ltd.
M-32 Market
Greater Kailash I
New Delhi 110 048 India

Printed in the United States of America

**Library of Congress Cataloging-in-Publication Data**

Main entry under title:

Child survivors and perpetrators of sexual abuse : Treatment
    innovations / edited by Mic Hunter.
        p. cm.
    Includes bibliographical references and index.
    ISBN 0-8039-7194-X (acid-free paper).—ISBN 0-8039-7195-8 (pbk:
    acid-free paper)
    1. Sexually abused children—Mental health—Congresses.
2. Sexually abused children—Rehabilitation—Congresses. 3. Teenage
sex offenders—Mental health—Congresses. 4. Teenage sex offenders—
Rehabilitation—Congresses. 5. Child sexual abuse—Treatment—
Congresses. I. Hunter, Mic.
RJ507.S49C48 1995
618.92'85836—dc20                                                    94-42211

This book is printed on acid-free paper.


95  96  97  98  99  10  9  8  7  6  5  4  3  2  1

Sage Production Editor: Tricia K. Bennett

# Contents

# *Foreword*

There is no more valuable resource to a society than children. Yet even the most conservative estimates suggest that the sexual abuse of children is all too common in the United States. As you read these words, there is a debate raging in both professional and public publications as to the validity of memories related to childhood sexual abuse. No doubt the debate will continue for years, even as children continue to be abused. Regardless of one's beliefs concerning the formation and recall of memories, there are several points on which most people can agree: There are children and adolescents who have been sexually maltreated, these children ought to receive treatment, and such treatment ought to be provided in an effective and efficient manner. As you will see, the contributors to this volume are dedicated to providing such treatment.

Although sexual abuse of children has existed since time immemorial, the serious study of the incidence and impact of such behavior has a very short history. Only 40 years ago, Weinberg's (1955) book, *Incest Behavior*, reported that incest took place in no more than one or two families per million. Unfortunately, we now know that sexual abuse is all too widespread. As we have opened our eyes to the suffering that results from sexual abuse, our simplistic views of what constitutes maltreatment and who perpetrates these acts have been shattered. We now know that much sexual abuse takes place in the home, that both men and women abuse children, and that children abuse other children. Just when we think that we have seen all there is to see, we gain a new, painful awareness.

This book will challenge many readers' concepts of the labels "victim" and "perpetrator." In doing so, it will cause discomfort, perhaps even anger. However, I believe that it will also lead to increased compassion for those who have responded to their own abusive pasts by repeating the pattern. Whenever I think about the labels "perpetrator" and "sex offender," I am reminded of a story told to me by a wise old man. He said that he had been present at a war crimes trial. A Jewish man who had been held in a death camp was led into the room to testify against a Nazi guard charged with killing the Jew's family and forcing him to put their still-warm bodies in the ovens to be burned. As the Jew's and Nazi's eyes met for the first time since the horrifying event, the Jewish man fell to the floor, thrashing and crying. The judge called for a recess so that the witness could compose himself prior to testifying. When the court was reseated, the prosecuting attorney spoke gently to the witness: "I'm sure this is very difficult for you. I imagine that you were overcome with hatred when you saw this monster before you," pointing at the accused Nazi. "No," responded the witness, "I expected to see a monster and to be filled with hatred. Instead I saw a man, just another person. And I was overwhelmed with the knowledge that if another human could do what he did, that I too could be capable of such acts, and it was more than I could stand to know about myself."

Part One, *Child Survivors,* begins with William Friedrich's chapter on the difficult but vital task of facilitating emotional regulation and impulse control in children who have been sexually abused. He not only provides a sound theoretical base for his treatment, but also provides the reader with practical treatment recommendations.

Unfortunately, not all those who experience sexual abuse have the opportunity to obtain treatment while they are children. Many do not become identified until they reach adolescence. Sally Cantor contributes a chapter on the specialized treatment of adolescents within the hospital setting. She provides the criteria for determining when inpatient treatment is appropriate and includes assessment techniques. She details the treatment process using her patients' own words to provide examples of the concepts she is explaining.

The final chapter in this part is contributed by Gayle Stroh. She focuses on what may be the most horrifying type of sexual maltreatment: ritual abuse. Because she is dealing with a controversial and emotionally charged topic, she easily could have overwhelmed the reader with graphic details. However, she is able to present her views with a detachment that makes the information very assessable to the reader, so that the valuable concepts are clear and are not overshadowed by the tragic histories of her patients.

Perhaps the most controversial topic within the field of sexual abuse is sexually aggressive children. Are they to be viewed as offenders or as victims? How they are labeled will affect how they are treated. Hendrika Cantwell opens Part Two, *Child Perpetrators*, by providing a cultural background for addressing this difficult issue. She invites the reader to look at our society and its impact on children, rather than merely focusing on the inappropriate behavior of the children.

Following Dr. Cantwell's overview, Jacqueline Jackson Kikuchi provides a model for identifying sexually aggressive children. She tackles the difficult task of defining the differences between normal child and adolescent sexual behaviors and behavior that ought to be considered abusive. She does so in a manner that is free of moralizing, a trap that befalls many authors who attempt this same task.

Once sexually aggressive children have been identified, how are they to be treated? Sandra Ballester and Frederique Pierre provide a treatment model for working with such youngsters. Their "monster" metaphor provides their young patients with a way to assume responsibility for their emotions and behaviors without also assuming the shame of a negative label.

The final chapter is provided by their colleagues, Diane Griggs and Armond Boldi, who describe a model for working with the parents of these children. Their program shows how the concepts described by Dr. Cantwell in her opening chapter can be put into practice to provide effective treatment.

I have been quite impressed by the knowledge and skills of these contributors. I am most grateful to them for their efforts in creating this book, as well as their attempts to heal the wounded young people that surround them. I know you will find what they have written useful in your clinical work.

Mic Hunter
St. Paul, Minnesota

# PART ONE

# Child Survivors

# Managing Disorders of Self-Regulation in Sexually Abused Boys

**William N. Friedrich**

I do not know about other therapists, but when I read reviews of the literature on the impact of sexual abuse, I am overwhelmed by the broad range of symptoms that has been potentially implicated (Kendall-Tackett, Williams, & Finkelhor, 1992; Urquiza & Capra, 1990). There is no single indicator of abuse, and the overt impact ranges from minimal to profound. Children could present in my office with symptoms that include compulsive behaviors, problems with sleeping, behavioral regression, and sexual acting out. How do practicing clinicians make sense of these behaviors? Once they have made sense of them, what are they supposed to do with them?

In a recent book, I suggested that three integrative perspectives could help therapists understand the impact of trauma (Friedrich, 1991): *attachment*, *self-regulation*, and *self-perspective*. Attachment is critical because it explains not only the disruption that the abuse brings to the child's relationship with the offender, but also why so many parents are unable to maintain a supportive presence prior to, at the time of, and after the abuse. The child comes into your office not expecting adults to be very helpful and feeling anxious, ambivalent, or out of control in your presence.

Dysregulation, the opposite of self-regulation, explains the lability and variability in the presentation of the sexually abused child. Children can change from session to session, presenting as overcontrolled one minute and undercontrolled the next. Some of these children seem as if they are being constantly bombarded by stimuli and have little defense against it.

> *Children who are dysregulated have difficulty with impulse control, emotional regulation, and problems with self-soothing.*

Finally, self-perspective takes into consideration the child's developing sense of self and how aspects of the abuse experience are integrated into this sense of self and become part of one's self-representation.

This chapter will focus on one of these three perspectives, *dysregulation.* Children who are dysregulated have difficulty with impulse control and emotional regulation, problems with self-soothing, and an inability to prevent feeling overly aroused or bombarded by thoughts or images of victimization. To some degree, disorders of self-regulation can fall in the externalizing behavior category (e.g., aggression) (Achenbach & Edelbrock, 1983). However, there are excellent materials available on working with these behavior problems (Patterson, Reid, Jones, & Conger, 1975). In this chapter, I will focus only on those conditions in which the child feels out of control or overly activated, and deals with his feelings in a more anxious or internalizing manner. Included in these behaviors are *sleep difficulties, dissociation,* and *panic.*

First, I will describe how trauma can be dysregulating, and then present theory related to emotional regulation and self-control. This will be followed by a discussion of examples from individual, group, and family therapy that can be used to enhance the child's self-regulatory capacity.

Having a theory to guide us as therapists is critical to good practice. One of the words that you will often see in this chapter is *integration.* Integration is a naturally occurring, developmental phenomenon that should occur in tandem with differentiation (Werner, 1948). Integration refers to the process in which different aspects of our selves become more smoothly and fluidly connected, allowing us to present as consistent individuals who know our thoughts and feelings. Both therapists and clients need to be integrated. Therapy is both an emotional and a cognitive task, and theory provides the cognitive dimension that needs to be integrated into therapy's emotional aspects. The degree to which therapists have integrated a useful theory into their ongoing practices will be reflected in how connected they feel to the clients they see and how attuned their therapeutic behaviors are.

## ■ The Role of Trauma in Dysregulation

Included in any list of behavioral sequelae of sexual abuse and/or other traumatic experiences are numerous examples that reflect dysregulation. Two other theories have already been suggested to understand the impact of sexual abuse, and both of them have at least one feature each that could be included in dysregulation (Briere, 1989a). These other perspectives are posttraumatic stress disorder and a traumagenic model developed by Finkelhor and Browne (1985). Included in Finkelhor and Browne's traumagenic model are several features that are dysregulatory. The primary feature is traumatic sexualization, which is the traumatic and precocious introduction of the child to sexual behavior. A second traumagenic factor also related to dysregulation is powerlessness. The sexually abused child most likely will have one or more out-of-control experiences as part of the abuse. Trauma can have a range of effects, including some that are neurophysiological, behavioral, and cognitive.

### Neurophysiological Effects

There has been an increase in literature that discusses the neurophysiology of trauma (Perry, 1993a, 1993b). Traumatic life experiences can have an impact on the development of the brain, specifically on those portions involved in mediating the stress response. During acute stress, the physiological response of the body is usually rapid and reversible. Prolonged stress can result in a more persistent, abnormal pattern, particularly if prolonged stress occurs during critical and sensitive periods of development. Perry states that "a child who is reared in an unpredictable, abusive or neglectful environment . . . will [have] a poorly organized, dysregulated CNS catecholamine system" (1993a, p. 17). This catecholamine system is involved in the regulation of a large number of processes, including affect, anxiety, arousal/concentration, impulse control, sleep, startle, autonomic nervous system regulation, memory, and cognition. These processes are reflected in all of the behaviors discussed in this chapter. In addition to a dysregulated CNS catecholamine system, some writers in this area suggest that after prolonged stress, neurotransmitter depletion can become a conditioned response, leading to excessive responsiveness (dysregulation, over-arousal) with subsequent, even minor, stressors (van der Kolk, 1988).

## Behavioral Effects

The neurophysiological response to trauma is difficult for the practicing clinician to quantify. However, behavior is observable and can be assessed. In this section, I present several types of behavior that can have a traumagenic component. These include sleep disorders, post-traumatic stress disorder (PTSD), attention-deficit hyperactivity disorder (ADHD), affective lability, compulsive behaviors, oppositional behavior, and dissociation.

### Sleep Disorders

Perry (1993a) has implicated the role of the neurophysiological system in regulating sleep. Other researchers have noted that children with behavioral and academic problems have far more sleep difficulties than do similar-aged children without problems (Morgan, 1990). There is also a developing literature on sexually abused children that identifies sleep disorders as a fairly consistent sequela, particularly in very young children (Hewitt & Friedrich, 1991).

Although sleep difficulties could be related to a child's depression following trauma, there are several other explanations for sleep problems. The traumatic experience may have caused an upset of the child's usual ability to self-regulate. The developing child gradually acquires the mastery of a number of different bodily functions, such as toileting and falling asleep, that require self-control. A child who has been traumatized can regress behaviorally, disrupting previous areas of self-control.

Van der Kolk (1988) suggested that state-dependent learning also has occurred around sleep. If the molestation occurs at bedtime, the child has on some level paired the sleep state with physiological arousal, which includes anxiety or the "flight" response.

### Posttraumatic Stress Disorder

Van der Kolk (1988) suggested that physiological disorganization sets the stage for an increased vulnerability to developing PTSD. Although PTSD does not characterize every child who has been sexually abused, and, in fact, is more likely to be characteristic of a child who has experienced more significant abuse by a close relative (McLeer, Deblinger, Atkins, Foa, & Ralphe, 1988), the PTSD conceptualization is very relevant here. PTSD symptoms fall into three areas: (a) recurring, intrusive recollections of the traumatic event; (b) persistent avoidance of stimuli associated with the trauma or numbing of general responsiveness; and (c) persistent symptoms of increased arousal characterized by hypervigilance, startle response, sleep difficulties, irritability, and anxiety. Although it is easy to see how symptoms from the first and third areas are related to feeling overwhelmed and dysregulated, numbing and avoidance are also associated with dysregulation. Problems with self-soothing or maintaining an internal equilibrium are reflected in either undercontrol or overcontrol. When children use overcontrol, they are using a maladaptive coping strategy to re-regulate themselves and to create some distance from the experience.

### Attention-Deficit Hyperactivity Disorder

ADHD is commonly thought to be biological in nature, and the role of arousal regulation has been examined in studies of its etiology. It is also far more common in males. However, there is some very compelling research that indicates that experiences in a young child's life are important and significant correlates of future ADHD-like behavior in young children (Jacobvitz & Sroufe, 1987). These researchers found that maternal interference and overstimulating care were related more to a diagnosis of ADHD by the age of 6 than were prenatal, postnatal, or other medical or physiological variables. Field (1985) has suggested that mothers are mediators of both soothing and arousal in children. If the mother and child are not synchronous, this may lead to physiological disorganization, which in turn can be reflected in extremes of under- and overarousal. Although sexual abuse was not directly examined in the Jacobvitz and Sroufe (1987) study, maternal interference and overstimulating care are models of interaction that also typify child molesters, who interfere with and overstimulate the child. Rather than simply ignoring ADHD symptoms that might be present in boys who present for treatment, conceptualizing their symptoms as part of a larger problem with self-regulation could be quite useful for treatment purposes.

*Emotional Lability/Reactivity*

The child who is quite labile in terms of his affect, demonstrating such behaviors as panic, sudden tearfulness, crying spells, and significant mood swings, is also a child who is reflecting difficulties with self-regulation. Panic is a basic emotion of fear that is a manifestation of an alarm reaction. Alarms can be either rational or irrational, and thus a cognitive component to affective lability is critical for its understanding. Variability in the child's display of affects suggests an internalizing behavior problem. Although variability is more likely to characterize sexually abused female children, it certainly is evident in male victims as well (Friedrich, Beilke, & Urquiza, 1988).

*Compulsive Behaviors*

Another internalizing behavior related to dysregulation is compulsive behaviors. This is not necessarily an anxiety state, but the behaviors are used to reduce anxiety. Compulsions are compensatory: Children attempt to alleviate their anxiety through compulsive and routinized behaviors. Although obsessive-compulsive disorders in children are quite unusual, and there is no clearly established link between traumatic events and the emergence of obsessive-compulsive behavior, I have seen a number of traumatized children who have, for brief periods of time, engaged in such compulsive behaviors as checking, washing, and counting. In fact, an item from the *Trauma Symptom Checklist-Children* (Briere, 1989b), which reads "Washing myself because I feel dirty inside," is endorsed more frequently by sexually abused children than by either nonabused children or psychiatric controls (Friedrich, 1991). Crittenden and DiLalla (1988) describe "compulsive compliance" as a manifestation of physical abuse characterized by an increased inhibition of disagreeable behavior. Another manifestation of dysregulation is overcontrol, as suggested in their paper.

*Oppositionality*

In a chapter specifically focused on symptoms in boys, we could spend a great deal of time on aggressive and oppositional behavior. However, oppositional behavior is not a unitary phenomenon. Oppositional behavior—which includes explosive outbursts, depression, and outbursts that are sandwiched between periods of appropriate behavior—can also reflect a child who is feeling dysregulated and who has experienced traumatic events (Perry, 1993b). In fact, Perry (1993b) states that children who have been traumatized often use an "alarm" reaction, characterized by freezing, that can become labeled as oppositional-defiant behavior. The child feels anxious after being provoked by a sensitized stimulus, may feel somewhat out of control, and is much less able to comply with requests. Parents may label this behavior as oppositional and interact with the child accordingly. Over time, this can set up a coercive pattern of interaction in which oppositionality becomes more entrenched (Patterson et al., 1975).

> *Behavioral manifestations of dissociation can include daydreaming, a seeming absence, and the child's disengagement from his social milieu.*

### Dissociation

A final example of behavioral sequelae of sexual abuse that is directly related to dysregulation is dissociation. The most common childhood equivalent of running away from a threatening situation is dissociation (Perry, 1993b), so it is readily understandable that trauma and dissociation are related. Behavioral manifestations of dissociation can include daydreaming, a seeming absence, and the child's disengagement from his social milieu. The more often the child has had to learn to disengage, the more likely he will use dissociation.

Referring back to integration, Braun (1988) defines dissociation as a disruption of memory and identity. In an integrated child, memory and identity are connected. Braun states that dissociation is a continuum of awareness, with dissociation occurring on any of four levels: behavior, affect, sensation, and cognition.

### Cognitive Effects

In addition to neurophysiology and behavior, dysregulation also occurs on a cognitive level. Trauma can affect how a boy thinks about himself. Persistent, intrusive thoughts can also be dysregulating to the child. Because some cognitive mechanisms are used as coping strategies, helping a boy think more accurately about the trauma can be helpful (Taylor, 1983). How a child interprets an abuse experience will vary depending on the child's age. Very young children are likely to routinely blame themselves for negative events, reflecting their egocentricity. Other children may search for meaning in the traumatic experience on their own, via a family member, or in therapy. If they are able to regain a sense of mastery over the event and over their lives generally, their resulting mastery, capacity to regulate, and self-esteem will be enhanced (Draucker, 1989).

Other cognitive manifestations of dysregulation include racing thoughts and depersonalization (e.g., "I don't feel real"). PTSD symptoms can also have a cognitive component, in addition to the affective and behavioral dysregulation described earlier. The lack of integration between thinking and feeling that is a result of trauma is also dysregulating and contributes to the child's variability and lack of predictability.

Thus far I have outlined a number of general reactions to the traumatic experience that are clearly reflective of dysregulation. In the next section, I will move beyond a description of the behaviors to examine how different theories explain the origins of dysregulation.

## ■ Theoretical Framework

As children grow and develop, they maintain a dynamic equilibrium both interpersonally and intrapsychically. The importance of regulatory, equilibrating mechanisms has long been recognized (Siever & Davis, 1985). Siever and Davis suggest that without equilibrium, dysregulation occurs. Dysregulation is related to a range of behaviors, including erratic and unpredictable behavior, reduced selective responsivity to stimuli, and a resting state that is more difficult to maintain and return to after arousal. Interestingly, Siever and Davis include depression as an example of a dysregulatory process.

Development is a complex process, as underscored in a paper by Braun (1988). He discusses four developmental strands: behavior, affect, sensation, and knowledge. These four processes function in parallel on a continuum over time. The degree to which these four developmental strands are *integrated* is directly related to the maturity and congruence of the personality. Braun states that traumatic events cause a separation among these levels, or a reduction in integration.

Preceding Braun's theory by 40 years is that of Werner (1948). He described two processes central to the formation of the self: *differentiation* and *integration*. Differentiation reflects the degree to which the organism becomes more complex and multifaceted over time. Integration reflects the degree to which these greater complexities become more interconnected and smoothly functioning. A fully mature organism would be an interesting mix of complexity, predictability, and diversity.

*Not everyone who experiences an event outside of the range of usual human experience will develop any one of several indicators of dysregulation.*

An important consideration in any dysregulation theory is the fact that not everyone who experiences an event outside of the range of usual human experience will develop any one of several indicators of dysregulation. The most well studied of these phenomena is PTSD. In a very useful review of the literature on the etiology of PTSD, Jones and Barlow (1990) discuss a number of models that have been developed to explain the development of PTSD. They believe that every model must take into consideration the fact that only a subset of individuals exposed to a dysregulating experience will later show symptoms. This is also very similar to the finding that sexual abuse does not have a unitary impact across children and that some individuals appear to be more immune to the effects of trauma (Friedrich, 1988).

Jones and Barlow (1990) begin with the fact that PTSD is primarily an anxiety disorder. In fact, PTSD is associated with both anxiety and depression, two other examples of dysregulation. They conceptualize anxiety as a cognitive-affective structure embedded in a feedback loop. The loop includes strong negative affect, consisting of perceptions of unpredictability and uncontrollability, as well as a preparatory coping strategy. Individuals become hypervigilant and narrow their attention to the source of potential threat. Jones and Barlow's model for the etiology of PTSD includes biological vulnerability to arousal, combined with a direct experience of a traumatic event coupled with intense, basic emotions (e.g., fear, anger, distress). This results in a learned alarm in which anxious apprehension is a common sequela. Anxious apprehension creates a psychological vulnerability to future traumatic events that, unless moderated by social support and adaptive coping, results in PTSD.

One of the psychological vulnerabilities that can contribute to the emergence of PTSD comes from attachment literature. Over the course of repeated interactions with a significant caregiver, the child develops an internal working model related to approach avoidance, self-regulation within the context of the relationship, and other critical elements pertaining to dysregulation. Many of the sexually abused children that I see have histories of rejection or traumatic lives (Friedrich, 1990). An impaired attachment relationship with even the nonoffending caregiver is often seen, and it is suggested by how positively and accurately the parent views the child (Everson, Hunter, Runyon, Edelsohn, & Coulter, 1989).

Earlier in this chapter, I mentioned Field's (1985) and van der Kolk's (1988) discussions of the moderating effect of a soothing maternal presence. The lack of a soothing and attuned parental presence will lead to anxious and ambivalent attachment in a boy. This makes him not only more vulnerable to PTSD and subsequent dysregulation, but also provides him with a model for behaving in a dysregulated manner. An anxiously attached child will show greater variabilities in anxiety and inhibitory behaviors than will a child who is securely attached. An ambivalently attached child, even prior to victimization, will exhibit less integrated behavior than will a securely attached child, alternating approach with avoidance in his interactions with caregivers.

The disrupted attachment present in the families of sexually abused boys is often multigenerational (Bowlby, 1984). Maltreating mothers were less likely to have a parent that they could turn to when they were children, and this situation exists into the present. In addition, the mothers of sexually abused children are more likely to be molested themselves than are the mothers of nonsexually abused children (Hewitt & Friedrich, 1991). A nonoffending female parent molested by a male would have to exert considerable extra effort to maintain a soothing and attuned relationship with her male child. Consequently, a sexually abused boy might have an even greater vulnerability for dysregulation following trauma.

A final feature of the model is the use of language as a moderator of the dysregulatory effects of trauma. The relationship between language and prosocial and well-modulated behavior has long been described (Mussen, 1975). Santostefano (1986) states that in reality, cognition and affect are present simultaneously. The degree to which both of these are integrated will reflect cognitive control and modulated behavior. When cognition and emotion are not present simultaneously, as suggested by Braun's (1988) model of dissociation, dysregulation can occur.

Related to language is a study on unexplained arousal (Zimbardo, LaBerge, & Butler, 1993). Zimbardo et al. compared the emotional, cognitive, and physiological responses of subjects experiencing induced physiological arousal with and without awareness of the source of their arousal. They found that unexplained arousal was associated with elevations in both self-reported and physiological measures of arousal, as well as negative mood states and misattributions regarding the nature of their arousal. Thus unexplained arousal carried with it physiological, behavioral, affective, and cognitive effects. These subjects were not victims of trauma, but the study is certainly relevant to sexual abuse in that arousal paired with an inability to talk about the source of the arousal is a common phenomenon with abuse.

Age-appropriate language is also associated with prosocial behavior and reduced aggressiveness in children. Boys are more likely to be immature in their language and thus more prone to dysregulation (Mussen, 1975).

In summary, the model that is most appropriate to understanding the cause of dysregulation in the sexually abused child is similar to Jones and Barlow's (1990), with several exceptions that are more applicable to children and to sexual abuse. According to Werner (1948), dysregulation results in differentiation and integration not proceeding apace. For example, a boy may be in foster care, all alone (a precocious form of individuation), and his behavior is variable, his feelings seem foreign, and he can't or won't think about his life (the absence of integration). This is a boy with an increased vulnerability to traumatic events. He is even more vulnerable if he is not growing up in a relationship where soothing and attunement are present (i.e., insecure attachment). The boy will have an internal working model of people not being available to him. Consequently, he will behave in an anxious or ambivalent manner when support is provided. Because he is a boy, language is also an important moderator that may be less effective. When language is present or permitted, the boy can understand the source of his trauma and he can search for more appropriate explanations for why he has been victimized and what that means about himself.

Now that the effects of dysregulation and a model to understand it have been articulated, we will turn in these last sections of the chapter to specific psychotherapeutic examples to help with dysregulation.

## ■ Treatment Considerations

By now, the reader should understand that dysregulation is not a random event. Although it is certainly related to the types of situations implicated in the development of PTSD, the literature reviewed thus far indicates that there is no linear relationship between a traumatic event and the experience of dysregulation or a persisting state of dysregulation. In fact, only some individuals who experience a traumatic event later show persisting indicators of dysregulation. When we think about therapy, we need to remind ourselves of this fact. We also need to determine ways in which the therapeutic process can mimic or enhance some of the natural coping resources of social support and the adaptive cognitions that are hopefully present or can be activated in the lives of young male victims.

### Individual Therapy

Individual therapy should have as a foremost consideration the structuring of the therapeutic process so that regulation is enhanced, the boy is not overwhelmed by the therapeutic process, and his behavior doesn't become so disruptive that therapy is terminated or disrupted. The strategies described in this next section will focus on structural components of the individual therapeutic process that enhance therapy as a soothing and reciprocal process.

I have long advocated that psychotherapy with sexually abused children benefits from some discussion of the sexual abuse experience (Friedrich, 1990). I still believe that disclosure is extremely important to the therapeutic process. However, the primacy of disclosure must be considered in light of what effect disclosure has on the child's life and behavior. Zimbardo et al. (1993) suggest that unexplained arousal is more negative than explained arousal. This adds scientific support for the need for disclosure. If there are parental proscriptions against the boy talking about his victimization, or if the boy perceives that talking about victimization will get him into trouble with his family, then disclosure may not be very useful.

Another phenomenon that I have noted is that boys who self-disclose very early in the therapy process—even too early, given the nature of their relationship with their therapists—may be simply responding to their complete dysregulation and feeling overwhelmed. They cannot make good decisions about what they say and to whom. Rather than immediately being gratified by a boy's self-disclosure within the first 10 minutes of the first session, the therapist automatically should be concerned by the degree to which the boy lacks self-control and subsequently is prone to dysregulation.

In my work with sexually abused children, I have noted that this early and inappropriate self-disclosure parallels the type of indiscriminate affection-seeking noted in physically abused children. They show poor boundaries and an impaired sense of self-other. In fact, as the child becomes more mature, and you as the therapist begin to mean more to him, he might back off from disclosure, even becoming embarrassed in your presence about what has happened to him. This speaks to a developing maturity and should be respected as much as possible. Embarrassment is an appreciation of the other and reflects the degree to which your perception of him now means something to him. Embarrassment makes it harder for a boy to ricochet through life with no thought for whom he is with. The embarrassed child is now finally thinking about how he might be perceived. In spite of these cautions, disclosure is still important.

> *Good therapy requires unconditional regard for the child.*

### Scheduling Disclosure

Good therapy, like good parenting, requires unconditional regard for the child as well as appropriate maturity demands. Disclosure about bad things that have happened to the child is part of the maturity demands. If the therapist explains to the child why this is important, and gives him an option about when and how he discloses his victimization, the therapist is being attuned to the child's needs and also creating movement for growth. The boy can realize that feeling and acting out of control are functions of having been abused. I am struck by how often sexually abused children do not link their behavior to their abuse experiences; frequently, they are simply reflecting their parents' lack of thought about their sons' behavior.

### Partitioning Sessions

Another technique to manage dysregulation is to divide sessions into work and play. This is suggested to the child, and the child has an opportunity to determine how much time is spent working on abuse and its related issues and how much time is spent on less directive and more play-oriented activities. Over the course of a 45- to 50-minute session, it is a rare child under the age of 12 who can talk about such negative events for the majority of the session. Again, partitioning sessions reflects attunement to the child's developmental level and as such helps to alter his internal working model of adults as being unsupportive and nonsoothing.

### Therapy as Reliable and Predictable

Every sexually abused boy who enters therapy should have the therapy process explained to him. The therapist needs to tell the boy what he will be doing and explain anything that he expects the boy to do. A predictable and reliable process can ease the child's anxiety as he begins to associate the therapist with feeling comforted and supported in a predictable manner.

### Relaxation/Hypnosis Training

Whether this is training that occurs within the session—and the boy then uses it between sessions—or whether the parent or foster parent has been recruited into this process depends on the boy's circumstances. But a therapist who is concerned about a child feeling overwhelmed should feel some urgency in giving the boy some additional strategies to reduce these feelings.

It is best to begin the relaxation or hypnosis training with younger children only after a concrete example emerges. Sometimes boys will become overtly anxious in the room, and then the introduction of a strategy (e.g., deep breathing) could be useful. Young children, particularly children who can't stop long enough to think about who they are, are rarely going to benefit from structured activities that are not tied to specific situations or events.

An important arena where relaxation and hypnosis can be useful is sleep and bedtime. The boy can imagine that he is in a safe place, he can learn how to breathe deeply, and he can learn how to gradually shut off his racing thoughts, pretending to use a dimmer switch. Another possibility is for the therapist to make a tape recording for the boy to help him learn self-hypnosis or relaxation more readily. The tape recording represents a token of the therapist and as such enhances the therapeutic attachment. Cognitive self-control strategies also can be quite useful and can further enhance the child's mastery. Self-control is useful with sleep, panic, and some features of ADHD (Anastopoulos & Barkley, 1992; Morris & Kratochwill, 1983).

### Preventing Spillover From Therapy to Home

It is important to realize that therapy can be dysregulating in spite of our best efforts. What is the impact of a boy who enters therapy and now is more difficult to manage? When his parent is already feeling overwhelmed, the boy is not going to be seen accurately, receive praise, or stay in therapy long. Spillover can be prevented by discussing some of the implications of therapy with the parent, preparing him or her for possible initial regression or increased arousal.

Partitioning of the sessions is useful to prevent spillover, but another technique that I use as well, particularly when we are talking about very dysregulating thoughts, is to circumscribe the therapy hour. I tell the child that he will return to the scary things we've been talking about only when I see him again. In the intervening time, he will be able to push the negative thoughts and feelings aside and act as if he has no worries or concerns; one could argue that this is a quasi-hypnotic intervention.

### Self-Soothing Techniques Emphasizing Control

The child may already have some ideas (reality or fantasy-based) about how to keep himself safe from further victimization. Hopefully, he has shared these ideas with you. The urge for mastery is very important and it is a rare child who doesn't have at least some mastery fantasies, some more realistic than others. But with all ages of sexually abused boys, there are techniques that can add to their sense of mastery, ranging from "monster spray" under the bed at bedtime, to drawing pictures of how they would fortify their houses if given the opportunity, to repeated episodes of imprisoning the molesters and recapturing them on escape. Be sure to keep the activities modulated, either through your pacing of the activities or your style of interaction.

### In-Session Aggression

A higher level of rough-and-tumble play is present in therapy with boys as well as therapy that returns to themes of sexuality and bowel-bladder processes. Paralleling or mirroring the child's aggressive play in the session might initially seem very useful for enhancing your relationship with him. If the boy continues to escalate in an aggressive manner, repeating the aggression in a stereotypic style, it is likely that your therapy is not helping the child learn self-regulation.

One of Terr's (1981) contributions to the literature on traumatic events and children is her concept of posttraumatic child play. Stereotypic and repetitive play that does little to enlarge on or elaborate the victimization experience should be circumvented, and the therapist needs to actively develop alternative themes and play behaviors. Sometimes that is done with language (e.g., identifying that the child's repetitive play is reflecting the abuse and its different characters) and other times it is done by distracting the child from the repetitive play. Whatever the case, monitor the child's play so that it does not become out of control and/or excessively aggressive.

### Therapist's Gender

Can a boy who has been molested by a male be treated by a male therapist? This is as useful a question as the one of female victims and male therapists. Take it as a given that children do discriminate between adults, particularly as they get older. This does not mean that there might not be some attendant anxiety within the relationship, and this is deserving of some attention. Again, language is a useful process here. I have spelled out, for example, ways in which I am different from other men in the boy's life and how I plan on conducting myself within the therapy session. Sometimes boys look curiously at me, sometimes they ignore me, and other times they act immediately (e.g., become relaxed), as if I have spoken directly to them and their fears.

### Medication

I am not a child psychiatrist and I do not profess to be an expert on psychopharmacology. However, there are numerous medications available that have been suggested as treatment adjuncts for some of the behavioral sequelae noted earlier, such as ADHD, panic attack, sleep problems, and explosive behavior. My philosophy is that if you have a good working relationship with a clinically astute child psychiatrist or pediatrician, and they know what they are doing with medication, there are times when medication can be helpful. Generally, an out-of-control child, who now behaves more attentively after medication, will have a positive outcome for both himself and his parents. On several occasions, stimulant medication has resulted in the child being able to focus more clearly on his victimization. Clinically, I have seen situations where children voice more suicidal ideation and self-deprecatory comments after the medication has taken effect. This is an unusual outcome and the material generated can be used therapeutically.

## Group Therapy

Although there has been no empirical determination that group therapy with sexually abused children is any more effective than any other modality, the clinical literature certainly supports its utility (Friedrich, 1990). Generally, I believe that group therapy is an effective means for boys to address the impact of past sexual abuse on their current functioning. The group therapist of sexually abused boys must take into consideration the fact that group therapy can be an overwhelming experience to some boys. In a manner similar to what I mentioned in the individual therapy session, the group therapist must make some effort to create safety within the group therapy environment (Scott, 1992).

### Careful Screening

If you begin with the belief that no therapeutic intervention is a panacea for every child, you will screen potential boy group members more carefully. Sometimes this is difficult to justify if you are in a small agency and the presence or absence of one boy can enable a group to begin functioning. However, children who have not acknowledged their victimization, or children who invite almost instantaneous peer rejection, are not going to be very good group candidates. I have also seen dysregulation occur if the child associates another child with his own victimization experience. In one group I led, three of the members knew each other because they had been part of a sex ring. One of the boys had actually been sexual with another one, but I was not aware of it when the group started. Once that was opened up as an issue, therapy could proceed, but I chose to do it with only the three boys as a group.

Larson and Maddock (1986) also suggest that the victim/victimizing continuum is an important subject in treatment considerations. Boys who primarily victimize should not be the predominant group members in groups consisting of boys who are ready victims or who have no sexual victimizing experience.

### Creating Safety

Scott (1992) suggests that safety can be created in several ways, such as using group rules that are created by the boys in the group and using a point system that rewards positive adherence to group rules and the expectation of safety. Structuring the group so that a disclosure about a boy's abuse experiences is delayed and the boy is given a clear assurance that the group will not make him immediately feel on the spot is also helpful.

### Boundary Making

This is another concept borrowed from Scott (1992), who describes a number of boundary development exercises used in groups with boy victims. Boys create safe spaces around themselves and use cardboard and masking tape to define boundaries in other activities. The activities allow both safety and structure so that rage does not become hurtful to others or overwhelming to the child himself.

### Structured Treatment

A number of therapists have developed week-by-week activities to be used in structured group approaches with sexually abused children (Mandell & Damon, 1989). The majority of the activities described in Mandell and Damon's manual are useful for both male and female children. Using exercises in a structured program can develop more organization and predictability within the session. The child can feel a sense of mastery as he completes the workbooks the group uses. Because of these features, structured approaches lend themselves to the prevention of dysregulation within the group setting. The caution I have is that structured exercises that are divorced from the child's behavior or that are directly tied to the child's experience may not be very helpful. A structured group approach that does not allow a sense of connection with the therapist, or does not help the child to learn from other children, will be less successful than one that addresses these natural relationship processes.

### Pair Therapy

Group treatment can occur without the more typically described number of six to eight members. In settings where large numbers of sexually abused boys are not available, or if you are working with boys who are quite immature and skill-building exercises are likely to be an important part of therapy, working with a pair of children can be quite useful. This approach to therapy has been described by Selman and Schultz (1990). In pair therapy, it is presumed that children can develop reciprocity and can profit from shared experiences. A long-range behavioral goal is that the boys in the pair can interact together for the length of the session in a reciprocal manner. Each child functions as if he were a friend to the other, and from this mode of interaction the boy can hopefully learn trust, reciprocity, and attunement, which he can take to other relationships. Although a long-term goal of Selman and Schultz's (1990) pair therapy process is that the therapist eventually is no longer present in the room with the two children, that is not an expectation that I have when I work with a pair.

### Family Therapy

Given what I have already mentioned in talking about internal working models and how that emerges as a function of attachment with parents, the family is certainly a critical arena in which the child has learned dysregulation and hopefully can learn some self-regulation. How does that come about? The basic philosophy is that if the parents feel anxious about the therapy process, or continue to be upsetting at home, the boy will reflect that.

### Reduce Overstimulation and Sexualized Behavior in the Family

Creating a sense of self-control in a child is related to creating safety in the family. Many parents do not realize how overstimulating they can be to the sexually abused child. Not only is this done through aggressive modeling, but it also occurs in open displays of sexual behavior or the tolerance of sexual behavior between siblings or siblings and parents. In a semiformal, longitudinal study of young people sexually abused as children, Burgess and her colleagues found that childhood physical abuse, parental modeling of aggression, and family blaming were related to persisting, socially deviant behaviors (Burgess, Hartman, & McCormack, 1987).

These findings illuminate the need for the family therapist of the sexually abused child to address physically punitive behaviors in the family as well as the modeling of sexualized relationships. This cannot be done simply by asking parents whether or not they behave in an aggressive or sexualized manner and then asking them not to do so. Many times, families may not know that they interact in aggressive or sexual manners. The therapist needs to look for direct examples of this in the therapy session so that the behaviors can be addressed in a clear but nonrejecting manner. Sexual behavior in a young boy will persist longest in families that are not good observers around sexual behavior and that, as a result, are likely to blur sexual boundaries.

### Goal Setting

Families who present with a sexually abused child are usually not aware of what is expected of them. They need to have therapy explained to them and the utility of therapy made quite concrete. Setting specific parent and child goals, and monitoring progress in achieving these goals, can help the family members identify with the therapy process and feel as if they are active participants. Examples of goal setting are included in Friedrich (1990) and will not be elaborated here.

In a related vein, a psychoeducational approach with families of sexually abused children actually has more utility than I had originally thought. Being an initial convert to structural and strategic therapy, I felt that using an educational and/or behavioral approach with families of young, sexually abused children did not seem either appropriate or very effective. However, the families I see have a multigenerational history of rejection. Educational and symptom-specific approaches that are clearly understandable to the parents go a long way toward helping them feel accepted, rather than rejected, and empowered in the therapy process.

### Family Rituals

Steinglass has studied the multigenerational transmission of alcoholism and has identified the presence of several buffering variables, including the presence of family rituals (Steinglass, Bennett, Wolin, & Reiss, 1987). Although helping a family that you see for only a few months to develop certain rituals may not be feasible, this concept is quite useful as a guide toward therapy. Members of families profit if they interact with each other in reliable and predictable ways. However you can enhance that, possibly around bedtime or meals, can go a long way toward helping the child feel as if his environment is at least predictable.

■ **Summary**

In conclusion, sexual abuse is related to the emergence of a broad spectrum of behavioral symptoms, some of which are best described as disorders of dysregulation. These include behavioral difficulties such as sleep disorders, PTSD, attentional difficulties, uncontrollable anxiety, and dissociation. A model for the development of dysregulation was suggested that included the traumatic experience, what the child had learned about relationships and self-soothing, and the enhancement of language as a coping strategy to deal with dysregulation. Finally, a number of therapeutic techniques derived from individual, group, and family therapy were suggested that specifically focus on preventing further dysregulation of the child victim as well as being sensitive to the regulatory and self-soothing needs of the boy.

**2**

# Inpatient Treatment of Adolescent Survivors of Sexual Abuse

**Sally Cantor**

Increasingly, psychiatric inpatient units for adolescents are recognizing the need to develop specialized treatment programs for adolescent survivors of sexual abuse. I began such programs at MeadowWood Hospital in New Castle, Delaware, in 1986 and at Northwestern Institute for Psychiatry in Fort Washington, Pennsylvania, in 1992. At MeadowWood Hospital, which has a strong commitment to treating survivors of sexual trauma, adolescent survivors average 42% of the hospitalized population. This number has been fairly consistent throughout the history of the hospital, although at times the majority of the female patients are survivors of sexual abuse.

For the purposes of this chapter, adolescent survivors will be referred to by the pronoun "she"; however, it is clear that males are also frequently sexually abused, and they are often overlooked.

Inpatient treatment for sexual abuse should be considered only after efforts have been made to address the adolescent's and her family's needs on an outpatient basis. Issues to address may include childhood sexual abuse, which can be incestuous or extrafamilial in nature. The patient may put herself at additional risk through substance abuse or provocative sexual behaviors. Ideally, outpatient therapy would involve the patient and her family in regular therapy with a therapist who is versed in sexual abuse issues. A further advantage is if multimodalities such as individual, group, and family therapies are included, which would allow for the integration of issues.

Inpatient treatment should thus be considered if outpatient therapy is unsuccessful and if depression, suicidal ideation or attempts, and/or risk-taking behaviors on the part of the adolescent increase. These risk-taking behaviors may include risky sexual behaviors, such as multiple sexual partners who may be significantly older than the adolescent; a pattern of sexual involvement only with individuals of a different race; or sexual experimentation by the adolescent who is too young to cope with sexual experiences. These behaviors are problematical because they often represent an intense dislike of self or an attempt to use sex to meet needs for closeness and intimacy. An attraction to sexual partners of a different race may reflect adolescent rebellion; it may also reflect the adolescent survivor's desire to connect with individuals who are racially different from her perpetrator(s) or whom she identifies as strong and powerful.

The adolescent often refuses to use any birth control and presents this refusal in terms of "I just don't believe in it." The adolescent is usually aware of the risks that unprotected sexual encounters pose, but minimizes them for herself. There may also be a strong desire to become pregnant to prove to herself that she has not been physically damaged by the sexual abuse, and out of a desire to give birth to a baby who will love her and give her life purpose.

These behaviors often result in a multiabuse pattern when an adolescent survivor is remolested or raped. This repeating of a sexual victimization process that began in childhood is often so dangerous to the adolescent that inpatient treatment should be considered. "Traumatic reenactment" is often connected with substance abuse, self-mutilation, suicidal ideation or attempts, and eating disorders; the adolescent's involvement in a cult may also be suspected. There may also be decompensation in the adolescent following court hearings related to the sexual abuse. This may occur regardless of a positive or negative outcome in court, owing to the individual's sense of personal responsibility, guilt, and shame. It is often these latter behaviors, rather than the sexual abuse, that are the presenting problems at hospitalization.

In seeking inpatient treatment for the adolescent survivor, the outpatient therapist and/or the patient's parents may not recognize the value of hospitalization in a facility where specific programming or groups exist for the survivor of sexual trauma. I believe that such programming is essential for the survivor because issues of shame are best processed in homogeneous settings with fellow survivors. The survivor also gains a sense of not being alone and can see that others are going through a similar process of healing and change. The survivor may experience many issues related to an impaired ability to trust, which is best addressed in a survivor group. Sexual abuse usually affects the acquisition of skills for living and may further result in chronic patterns of inappropriate sexualized behaviors, continuing all the way to sexual perpetration.

> *Sexual abuse may result in chronic patterns of inappropriate sexualized behaviors.*

## ■ Aspects of Inpatient Treatment

When establishing an inpatient treatment program within an adolescent unit, the first issue to consider is safety. It is essential that boundaries are clearly protected and defined between staff to staff, patient to patient, and staff to patient.

Parameters must be clearly defined regarding touching of patients, and under what circumstances. Clear boundaries should also be established to protect patients' rights to bodily privacy and at nighttime. In hospital settings, staff often need assistance in keeping their own issues separate from the patients, and the staff's self-disclosure both to the patient and the patient's family ideally should be kept to a minimum. For an example, please see Appendix A, MeadowWood Hospital's policy regarding "patient involvement and socialization policy."

I believe that ideally there should be a "nontouching" policy in which neither staff nor fellow patients touch each other. This assists in maintaining safety and also inhibits patients from using touch to meet all their needs.

Having clearly defined and enforced policies regarding touch are crucial when issues of needing to physically restrain patients are considered. In both hospitals mentioned, physical restraints are used when patients exhibit out-of-control behavior and attempt to injure either themselves or others. In some situations, after unsuccessful attempts to help the patient regain self-control, the patient must be forcibly carried to the "quiet room" for purposes of restraint. (In my experience, both hospitals have special rooms that are physically safe, where patients who are out of control can be placed until they are in control again.) In extreme situations where the patient is out of control, she is physically restrained on a bed, face down, by leather straps placed around her wrists and ankles. She is never left alone by staff. The goal is to help her make a contract to be safe, and then the restraints are gradually removed. In all situations, the patient should be advised that she is out of control and should be given the option of walking to the quiet room with staff. Attempts are then made in the quiet room to help the patient regain control.

If restraints are needed, then same-sex staff should be involved if possible. Using same-sex staff helps the survivor to not feel retraumatized if she was molested by an opposite-sex perpetrator. For the survivor who was abused by a same-sex perpetrator, it is helpful for staff of the same sex to verbalize for the patient that they are touching or holding the patient to keep the patient safe, and are not abusing the patient.

In most cases, due to staffing considerations, using staff of the appropriate sex is not possible. Same-sex staff should be used around the patient's torso. Because the process of being "held down" may result in the survivor reexperiencing the abuse, staff should be aware of the secondary gains that the survivor may experience during restraints. Ending restraints or confinement in the "quiet room" should include discussing with the patient the reason she was conducted to the quiet room and put under restraint, hearing her explanation of what triggered the out-of-control episode, and discussing what can be done to keep such experiences from recurring. If the patient is receiving secondary gains from being restrained, addressing them should become a priority in both individual and group therapies.

Hospital adolescent units also need clearly defined dress codes for staff and patients in which tight-fitting or sexually provocative clothing is not permitted. Patients also should not be permitted to wear clothing that advertises drugs or sex. Furthermore, efforts should be directed toward keeping the unit safe from materials that patients can use for self-mutilation. This may include having the patient remove all jewelry, including pierced earrings, and carefully monitoring the use of pencils, pens, staples, and paper clips. Hair sprays, deodorants, razors, and curling irons also can be used for self-mutilation and/or for suicidal behavior. Having such policies in place creates a safe environment where individuals can work on "survivor issues."

Adolescent hospital units must also develop a zero tolerance for sexual contact among patients, which includes confronting patients on any provocative sexual behavior. With safety established, the process of identifying patients who need specific treatment related to sexual abuse can begin.

## ■ The Sexual Abuse Assessment

A thorough assessment (refer to Appendix B) to evaluate if a patient was sexually traumatized is often warranted even if the abuse is disclosed at the time of admission to the hospital. The assessment is useful to determine the presence or absence of sexual abuse, the extent of the trauma, and issues related to mandatory reporting of sexual abuse. The individual performing a sexual abuse assessment should be highly knowledgeable about sexual abuse, its impact on adolescents, and the behaviors consistent with adolescents who have been sexually abused.

Prior to actual interventions with the patient, the sexual abuse therapist should make use of information obtained about the patient at the time of admission. During the admission assessment, intake personnel are encouraged to ask about the possibility of physical and sexual abuse when they ask about other issues, including depression, oppositional behavior, suicidal behavior, eating disorders, and school and family problems. It is my experience that patients often initially deny sexual abuse due to the stress of being admitted to a hospital, but some may disclose at this point. At intake, the patient and the patient's family should sign a statement that describes their rights regarding confidentiality and how these rights may be amended if there are disclosures of abuse that warrant reporting to those state agencies mandated to investigate child abuse.

Prior to meeting with the patient, the evaluator should confer with staff to see how the patient is handling sleeping in a hospital room, sharing a room, and maintaining privacy with a roommate. Issues related to needing the lights on or the bedroom door open should be noted. The patient's reaction to a body search, a routine admission procedure in most psychiatric hospitals, and to physical exams and blood work may be significant. Survivors often have intense reactions to these procedures because of their intrusive nature and the subsequent feeling of being out of control.

The actual assessment is usually done when the doctor requests a patient evaluation from the sexual abuse therapist. The significance of this lies in insuring that the psychiatrist has also noted indicators that may lead to a disclosure of abuse. The interview is usually more successful after the patient has made an initial adjustment to the psychiatric unit and is beginning to accept being hospitalized.

Efforts should be made to secure an interview setting that provides safety for both the patient and the evaluator. Interviews should *not* take place in a patient's bedroom because of the connection between bedrooms and sexual abuse/sexual contact. Psychiatric hospitals often have limited interview space, but it is better to delay the sexual abuse assessment than to interview inappropriately in the patient's room. The patient should be given as much control as possible during the interview, including having the door to the interview room left open or shut.

Efforts should be made to normalize the interview, and I usually introduce myself by stating, "My role here at the hospital is to talk with patients about different types of abuse. I talk to most patients." This prevents the patient from feeling singled out or isolated. Because survivors usually have impaired abilities to trust, it is also useful to explain that some abuse must be reported to child protection agencies, so that the patient does not feel betrayed if a disclosure is then made and reporting is indicated. Although this may delay disclosure for some patients, it is preferable to the patient's feeling betrayed by not being so advised. Issues related to reporting often need to be explored in treatment.

*The evaluator should ask the patient to define physical, sexual, and emotional abuse.*

Even if there is an initial denial of any abuse, the evaluator should ask the patient to define physical, sexual, and emotional abuse to ensure that the patient has some familiarity with what is being discussed. The patient is then asked to give examples of different types of abuse and whether they relate to the patient. Regarding physical abuse, the evaluator should look for connections between physical abuse and discipline within the family. I have found it significant to explore this area more fully when physical discipline has involved spankings or beatings on the buttocks beyond age 10, and if other family members are required to watch. Patients often do not find such experiences abusive and need help in understanding how it may have affected them.

In looking for indicators of sexual abuse within the family, the evaluator ought to look for indications that boundaries are not respected within the patient's home. These may include asking if family members knock before opening a closed door, and if there are doors on all rooms. I have been struck by the number of homes where incest occurs in which there are no doors for bathrooms or the child's bedroom. This exploration of what abuse means should take place prior to asking the patient specifically about herself.

The patient ought to be asked about her comfort level with family members, past and present, and to identify the reasons for any discomfort. The patient also should be asked about her experiences with caretakers and baby-sitters. The parents' history of substance use/abuse and sexual abuse should be explored because this may also indicate issues within the family. Parents who are abusing substances may put their child at risk to other substance abusers or may indicate impaired abilities to control their own impulses. Also, parents who have experienced incestuous sexual abuse in their childhood may not protect their child from the same abuser. There is a myth that individuals become too old to abuse, but it is not uncommon to discover that a child has been abused by the same individual who abused her parent.

As part of the evaluation, it is important to inquire about the patient's knowledge of and decisions about sex. Where did the patient learn about sex and from whom? These questions may elicit information about inappropriate sexual experiences. Inquiries should also be made about whether the patient is sexually active and, if so, how comfortable she is with her sexual behavior. I have learned that many patients interpret the term *sexually active* to mean within a recent time frame and will answer negatively if they are not currently involved in a sexual relationship. Information should be obtained about if and when the patient lost her virginity and about her decision to do this. Of particular concern is the patient who did so under the influence of alcohol or drugs, or says that the experience was not good for her. Inquire about the number of sexual partners and their ages. Patients who appear to have numerous sexual partners or partners who are much older may be putting themselves at risk. For the same reasons, inquire about birth control and whether it is possible for the patient to be currently pregnant. Most hospitals do routine pregnancy tests on female patients at admission. These tests need to be repeated if the results are negative and the patient was having unprotected sex up to 10 days before admission. There also appears to be a correlation, in my observations, between sexual abuse and adolescents who refuse to practice safe sex or who become involved in other high-risk behaviors.

The patient is next asked to identify any times in her life in which she felt she was "used" sexually. I have observed that many patients feel more comfortable being asked about "being used" than about being sexually abused. This may assist the patient in disclosing incidents of being raped or taken advantage of at parties while under the influence of drugs and/or alcohol. Usually there has been no previous disclosure because the patient considers herself equally responsible for using drugs, sneaking out of the home, skipping school, or other behaviors that she knows are unacceptable to her parents or society.

I also look for indicators of dissociation and inquire about dreams of being sexually abused. I often encounter adolescent patients who may deny any experiences with abuse but claim to have no memories prior to a certain age; such patients should be carefully monitored for dissociative experiences. This is clearly not sufficient indication of being abused.

There should also be discussion as to whether the patient has a history of self-mutilation, abusing or hurting animals, or fire-setting. Although positive responses to the above do not definitely indicate abuse, they are indicators that abuse should be suspected.

If sexual abuse is disclosed, the evaluator should ask about other perpetrators. It is my experience that adolescent survivors may focus on one particular perpetrator and may minimize the impact of other perpetrators. (Part of the focus of sexual abuse therapy becomes helping the patient integrate all experiences with perpetration.)

If the disclosed abuse involves a same-sex perpetrator, it is important to inquire about the impact on the patient's sexuality. Patients often need help in accepting that this does not change who they are sexually. Special consideration must be given to assisting male survivors who are more likely to be abused by same-sex perpetrators. Again, efforts should be made to explore the impact of the abuse on their sexuality and how the abuse affects their relationships and dating. I have observed that many male survivors who were abused by another male defend against injuries to their sexual identity by disclosing extensive sexual relationships with females.

Finally, the patient should be reminded of the mandatory reporting laws and the time frame for reporting. The therapist should help the patient to accept the need to involve the parents. If a parent is the perpetrator, efforts should be made to explore the patient's safety. At this point, the patient can be referred to specialized inpatient treatment for survivors of sexual abuse. In both hospitals, this can involve a combination of individual, group, and art and/or movement therapies.

## ■ Inpatient Survivor Groups

Regarding treatment, the focus of survivor groups tends to be on clarifying issues of guilt and self-blame. The group becomes a place to look at these issues and for group members to challenge the reasons behind the guilt. The impact issues outlined by Frances Sarnacki Porter, Linda Canfield Blick, and Suzanne M. Sgroi in "Treatment of the Sexually Abused Child," in Sgroi's (1982) *Handbook of Clinical Intervention in Child Sexual Abuse,* include guilt, fear, depression, and feeling damaged. Other issues include exploring how being abused affects sexuality.

Inpatient programs that are functioning well can draw on the hospital milieus to address issues of sexuality. It is important for the sexual abuse therapist to know how the patient is viewed by staff and how the patient relates to her peers. Owing hopefully to close monitoring in the hospital, it should be known if the patient is attempting to become involved in a sexual relationship with a peer, sneaking into a peer's room, writing notes of a sexual nature to peers, or otherwise attempting to act out issues related to abuse. The patient needs to be confronted by staff and her peers in general and told that her hospitalization is to address issues, not to have a relationship. The patient should be held accountable, and encouraged to describe her behavior to the group and to identify the needs she is attempting to meet through sexual contact. Such behavior is common with both male and female survivors.

In a good inpatient sexual abuse treatment program, survivor groups are viewed as having the same merit in assisting the patient's treatment as family therapy and individual sessions with the psychiatrist. Therefore, an early goal in program development is insuring that other therapists accept this view. It is equally important that the patients realize that this is a crucial part of their inpatient treatment.

Differing from some outpatient groups, inpatient survivor groups need to be open groups in which new patients are admitted after admission to the psychiatric unit and after the sexual abuse assessment.

Included are patients who both minimize their issues or who deny being affected by their abuse. Usually the group process helps these patients to view differently their experiences with abuse. In most cases, patients who are sexual perpetrators or who cannot maintain the confidentiality of their peers should be excluded from the group. In some cases, where the adolescent sexual perpetrator has already done extensive work on perpetration issues prior to attending the group, admission to the group may be appropriate. Patients who are too limited cognitively to understand the group should also be excluded.

Confidentiality is often a main issue to explore in survivor groups. Patients have experienced such a betrayal of their trust by their perpetrators that it is often very difficult for them to accept and believe that their peers or the group therapist will handle their issues any differently. It is essential that "breaking confidentiality" be dealt with in general in the psychiatric unit and in a serious manner. At Meadow-Wood Hospital, for example, breaking confidentiality is as serious as becoming threatening or assaultive. This is explored in the group and exceptions to confidentiality are discussed, including the fact that information about the patient may be shared with her treatment team (other professionals involved with her treatment) and recorded in charts. The patients are reassured that nothing they say will be shared with other patients, which is often their major concern. Patients also are advised that admission of suicidal behavior or thoughts, or any other self-destructive behavior, such as a plan to escape from the hospital or to resume using drugs, will be recorded, as well as additional disclosures of being victimized. As the group develops, it is helpful for a member of the group to explain "confidentiality" and then the group therapist can comment on any inaccuracies. Confidentiality discussions, coupled with issues related to trust, surface regularly in such groups.

Other decisions to consider when developing a survivor group is whether the group will be coed or same sex, as well as issues related to the sex of the therapist. At MeadowWood Hospital, survivor groups for adolescents are same sex, whereas at Northwestern Institute, the groups are coed. In the former, greater staffing patterns allow for same-sex groups. Adolescent male survivors often have been identified as functioning on such different developmental levels that group processing becomes difficult in a coed group. It often appears that adolescent males' sexual development is arrested because of the abuse, and maintaining them in same-sex groups, or providing individual therapy, seems more beneficial. Initial issues relate to becoming self-assertive and identifying the impact of their abuse on their sexual identity; these are often best addressed in a male survivor group. At Northwestern, where my time is more limited, the groups have been coed.

Patients appear to recognize that there is value to both types of groups. I have observed that issues related to being sexually out of control as a result of abuse are harder for patients to address in coed groups. It is observed that male patients often find it easier in coed groups to explore issues related to whether being sexually abused changed them and made them gay.

Ideally, survivor groups should have a cotherapist. One therapist often cannot handle all the issues being addressed, and nonverbal material can be missed. It is also helpful if the therapists are not directly involved in the patient's day-to-day life, such as administering consequences for behavior, because this can take on too much weight in the group.

Group leaders must be very clear regarding what they will or will not disclose about themselves. Regularly in group, usually at a time when group members are feeling defensive or unsafe, they confront me with, "Sally, we need to know if you've been sexually abused, because if you haven't, you can't help us." Other issues they ask about include whether the therapist has been raped, beaten by a boyfriend/husband, or is/is not a virgin. I explain, "I'm not going to answer your questions because I would never use your group to deal with my issues. If I have issues, I will go to an adult group." There appears to be an advantage to letting transference take place without knowledge of the therapist's issues.

I learned a valuable lesson about not self-disclosing, after a particularly grueling day. The theme in the survivor group was that every woman gets beaten at least once by her husband/boyfriend. When asked directly about this, I disclosed that I had never been beaten. It was soon clear that the group didn't believe the disclosure and that it didn't matter anyway.

Because inpatient survivor groups need to accommodate new admissions as they enter the hospital, they therefore need to be open-ended. This differs from outpatient groups, where the survivor may contract with the therapist to attend a certain number of groups or cycle of groups. Certain rituals have evolved to help old group members accept the addition of new group members, and they are outlined below.

### Explaining the Group

Old group members take turns explaining the purpose and the rules of the group to new group members. This includes defining membership in the group as being for patients who have been sexually abused, raped, and "incested" (a 14-year-old's term). Gradually, the purpose of the group has expanded to include patients who have been sexually harassed at school or who have "sex for the wrong reasons" or "too much sex." I have found it significant that the members define the group from day to day according to what they wish to address. The rules governing confidentiality are also reviewed as new members enter the group. This continuing explanation adds to the need to always build trust in the group.

### Survivor Versus Victim Group

New members are told that the group is called a survivor group and not a victim group because "we are not victims any more. We got through the abuse and now survived it." This appears to help group members feel hope. As therapy progresses, group members are asked to identify when they are behaving like survivors and when they are behaving like victims, and also to identify where they see themselves on a path of moving from victim to survivor. (For an alternative view on the use of these terms, see Hunter & Gerber, 1990.)

### Group Introductions

New members are told that in every group they will be expected to explain why they are in a survivor group—not why they were admitted to the hospital. This means that if the patient is in the group three times a week, then she gives her introduction three times. Patients are told that the introduction should include their name, age, and a brief description of why they are in the group, including their ages when the abuse took place. A typical explanation might be "My name is Susan. I'm 15, and I'm in this group because I was molested by my father from ages 4–12. Something else happened when I was little with a female babysitter, but I don't remember, and my friends tell me that I had sex with four guys at a party. I don't really remember, because I was so high. I don't really think it was rape."

Regarding introductions, patients are told that they can choose not to do their introduction if they give their reasons to the group. Mary might say, "My name is Mary, 14, and I don't want to do my introduction because I'm too embarrassed," or "I don't trust someone in the group," or "it gives me flashbacks." Following introductions, there is a brief discussion of how group members handled doing introductions and a recognition of which members shared new information.

Regularly, the group leaders are asked, "Why do we have to do our introductions every time we meet even if there aren't new members?" The explanation given to the members is that by doing the introduction, they can increase their comfort level with what has happened to them. In addition, as the group member gains comfort in the group, the introduction is usually expanded to include additional experiences with abuse. Equally important is noting when group members exclude information from their introductions, and exploring their reasons.

### The Empty Chair

There is always an empty chair in the group. The purpose of the empty chair is to serve as a reminder to patients that the group always has room for a new member, and that when a member leaves, the group will think of her on the empty chair. The chair is not a "gestalt chair" nor does it represent perpetrators. Group members are often relieved when they realize that they are not expected to talk to the chair. In one of the hospital programs, the patients named the chair "Faith" because they had faith that their lives would get better.

These initial rituals appear to be very important in allowing cohesiveness to build and establishing a safe, consistent way for group to begin.

Certain themes appear regularly in survivor groups that must be addressed by the group to move forward. Many of these themes connect with the patient's desire not to explore the issues of abuse, and include the following.

*"My abuse is not as bad as everyone else's, so I'll just listen."* The group needs to be able to convey to all members that *any* abuse is bad and that the group has time to address everyone's abuse. The patient needs further help in recognizing that she is being overresponsible for others and underresponsible for herself. She is asked how this ties in to her caring for her parents, siblings, and friends, and whether there is a pattern to this. This pattern of over/underresponsibility often comes

up when the patient begins to recognize that she is having sex with boyfriends because she is afraid if she says no, she will hurt their feelings. The therapist must be prepared to intervene in situations where patients compare "who had the worst abuse." Again, the focus should be on allowing all group members to explore their issues related to abuse, not weighing the level of abuse.

*"What happened to me wasn't rape"* . . . because *"I was drunk,"* . . . *"he said he was sorry,"* . . . *"we had sex before,"* . . . or *"it was a family member."* There often needs to be careful exploration by the group of what constitutes rape and the definitions of terms. Patients regularly minimize what happened to them if they perceive themselves as having done something wrong, such as running away or drinking. It is important to ask, "Is it Suzie's fault that she got raped when she ran away?" As the group looks at the issues, the members need to recognize that Suzie didn't run away to get raped. It is helpful to have members describe a rape situation in which they wouldn't feel responsible. They often describe a situation in which they are 90 years old, wearing a long flannel nightgown and sleeping in a locked house when a stranger breaks in. The group leader needs to challenge and ask about how often this scenario happens, and acknowledge that most victims are known to their rapists. It is often helpful for patients with these issues to look for articles in the newspaper describing rape.

The group needs to help patients recognize that drinking, abusing drugs, and running away may be self-defeating decisions for them to make, and that they have to take responsibility for their decisions and identify other changes they need to make. Each member needs to recognize that staying a survivor will be very difficult if she continues to drink and take drugs.

*"It [the abuse] never bothered me until you made me think about it."* This is common with patients who have repressed feelings related to the abuse but still have some memories, as well as with patients who have repressed both memories and feelings but the abuse is documented by others (e.g., those patients who state, "I don't remember it at all. My mother told me about it."). The task of the therapist and group members is to help these individuals identify current behaviors that may be linked to their abuse. It is also crucial to educate the entire group about processing traumatic events and that it is impossible to deal with painful memories and experiences without feeling pain. The patients

often visualize the traumas, which they claim do not affect them, as being like a cancer, which shows no indication of its presence on the outside. It grows and spreads, and finally erupts.

*Patients may never forget the abuse, but they can learn to contain the memories.*

"*My goal is to forget about my rape, molestation, and/or what my father did to me.*" This is frequently heard in group therapy, and the desire to forget must be challenged. Patients need to recognize that they may never be able to forget the abuse, but they can learn to contain the memories so that they are not overwhelmed. It is often helpful in group for patients to reflect on how much of their bodies are consumed with their abuse issues, and what would happen if they could let some of their feelings flow out. They are then asked to identify what good feelings or experiences could take their place.

"*I'm not here for sexual abuse issues*" . . . "*I'm focusing on substance abuse issues, or family problems, or depression*" . . . "*I'll work on sexual abuse issues another time.*" Patients need help in realizing that all of their issues are intertwined and that their recovery means integrating these issues. In a hospital with good trauma-healing programs, this means that family therapy, substance abuse treatment, and other therapies do not conflict with survivor groups, and all issues are integrated.

On the other extreme from the patients who avoid seeing the connection between all their issues are the patients who state, "I only have survivor issues." These patients need help in understanding that they have more than one issue to address. They also need help in identifying these other issues and in integrating these issues with their survivor concerns. This is often done in other group therapies where the patient considers family problems, school problems, and so on, and where the patient is reminded that her sexual abuse issues ought to be discussed in survivor group, leaving time in other therapies to address other issues.

Some patients' disclosures are not believed by significant others in their lives. This may lead to the survivor thinking, "The police and/or my parents didn't believe me, so why should you?" Such patients may need to explore issues related to why they are not believed, such as a history of lying. They may recognize that the group may give them hope. Parents not believing the patient is something that needs to be explored in family therapy, often with the sexual abuse therapist supporting the patient. Issues related to "false memories" need to be identified if this is what the parents suspect. The patient explores with the parents, in the presence of the therapist, her disclosure of sexual abuse, and the therapist explains to the parents how this connects to the patient's behavior. MeadowWood Hospital has prepared a pamphlet that lists indicators of sexual abuse, which is helpful to parents in identifying which behaviors connect with their child.

The final task of the group is to help patients recognize and accept that inpatient survivor groups can offer them help only in beginning the process of healing. Not all of their issues will be resolved while in the hospital, and they need to realize the value of continuing in outpatient survivor groups. Some patients may respond to this by rushing to disclose too quickly, and those that do need help in pacing themselves and taking "baby steps." The group can support patients in doing this. Patients often believe that they need to talk about every specific memory of abuse, and they do this without processing the memories or the feelings. As a therapist, I find it is often difficult not to have the opportunity to work with the survivor in a long-term relationship on the issues.

Patients may also use the survivor group to explore issues related to their loss of virginity, if this occurred as a result of abuse. In general, patients in the survivor groups at both MeadowWood and Northwestern believe that if their virginity was "taken" from them as a result of molestation or rape, they can make a conscious choice to "give it up" or "make love" for the first time with someone else. It is helpful in the groups for patients to explore what factors need to be in place before they have sexual contact. Sexual behavior tends to be an area where survivors are most likely to experience setbacks, or what the patients refer to as *survivor slips*. A survivor slip is a time when the patient made an inappropriate decision about having sexual contact or became involved in other risk-taking behaviors. The patients ought to recognize that if they slip, they can recover from it and not regress to a continuing pattern of inappropriate behavior. This is also part of the work that survivors can do in connecting their behaviors to issues of abuse.

Patients also explore how being abused affected their childhood, which may include feeling that they never got to play or to be carefree. They may also identify that as children, they were never able to relax when they slept because they rarely felt safe from perpetration. They need to identify how they can salvage what remains of their childhood. Elsewhere in the hospital, but often in group too, they need to be encouraged to play.

Although wanting to see adolescents in general refrain from having sexual intercourse, I have found this to be an unrealistic expectation. It is therefore crucial either as part of the group or elsewhere in the hospital for the patients to receive competent sex education. Many female survivors are highly resistant to using contraceptives out of a fear of having a pelvic exam—they view it as being molested again. When this theme comes up in group, I often bring a speculum to group to help patients learn more about exams.

Efforts should be made in the hospital to also help male patients assume responsibility for birth control. Educating them in the risks of unprotected sex is helpful, and they can also benefit from exploring how their lives would change if they fathered a baby. For the male survivor who experiences sexual abuse as robbing him of his masculinity, the idea of fathering a baby may initially appear satisfying. This should be discussed fully in group.

The idea of whether the survivor needs to forgive her perpetrator is also addressed in group. Patients must identify what has changed in their relationships with their perpetrators in order to forgive them. They need to explore how this idea of forgiveness ties in to their religious beliefs. I believe that a survivor does not owe forgiveness to her perpetrator unless the perpetrator has apologized, made amends, or unless the survivor's rage is getting in the way of her healing. (For an alternative view on the issue of forgiveness, see Hunter, 1990.)

## ■ Nontraditional Therapy Tools

Ideally, the sexual abuse therapist should make use of his or her imagination and other skills when assisting patients. Adolescent patients often get tired of talking about their abuse and need to explore its ramifications in other ways. The following are examples that have worked.

*Survivor boxes* are introduced to the group when there are issues related to lack of trust or when the group feels overwhelmed with trying to process abuse issues. Patients are instructed to make a box of any style or size that they wish. Materials are provided for them in the group. They are told that there must be a way of getting into the box and securing it. They are told that whatever they put on the *outside* of the box, they will need to share with group members. Whatever they put *inside* the box is their choice to share or not.

When the box is finished, which may take the full time for the group, patients are encouraged to store memories or feelings inside the box by writing poems, stories, words, or by cutting pictures out of magazines. In subsequent groups, patients are asked to share from the outside of their boxes, and then to take risks and share something from the inside of their boxes. Making a survivor box is also useful to do in individual therapy with survivors.

*Commonality sheets* involve spreading a large sheet of butcher's paper on the floor and having each member claim a space on the sheet to write down every word that comes to her mind about being a survivor. Patients are then given an opportunity to look at other members' lists and compare.

*The survivor quilt*, adapted from the AIDS quilt, is an attempt to allow patients to leave something of themselves behind for future group members. My quilt came from "borrowing" sheets from the hospitals and allowing patients to either draw a picture or write something on the sheet that relates to their survivor issues. The patient signs her first name only to protect confidentiality. This is done with embroidery crayons. The design is then ironed. The sheet can be hung out or displayed when the group meets. The sheet also conveys that the patient is not alone by identifying how many survivors there are.

Similarly, group members may wish to write *survivor prayers* as a way of introducing spirituality to the group. Group members who are looking for a spiritual connection often write prayers as homework to share in the group. A prayer written by a 15-year-old survivor is "Dear God, Let me use this group to heal and be safe. Guide me towards people who will help me and not hurt me." A particular prayer can be used in group as long as it serves a purpose for the members.

*Survivor journeys* are a movement exercise in which the group is asked to view the group room as their life. One wall is identified as "being victimized," and the wall across as "being a survivor." Each patient is asked to create the obstacles to being a survivor that must be overcome on her journey. The patients are asked to use fellow patients as the obstacles and to either climb or go through them. Each patient must label what the obstacles are, such as parents not believing, being addicted to sex, and so on.

*Time lines* are an exercise in which the patients are given paper and asked to graph their lives, showing the ups and downs they experience.

They typically use yarn, which they glue to the paper to make the graph. They are asked to include all of their abuse, even if there were experiences with abuse that they consider insignificant. They are also encouraged to chart good experiences that happened to them. They then share their time lines in the group.

*Anonymous disclosures* are used in groups that appear to be shame based and where members have a difficult time discussing what is really bothering them. Patients are given paper and asked to write anonymously something they would like to share with the group. The group leader collects the papers and reads aloud the responses. Members comment on what is read.

*Puppets* are useful with younger groups and can be made out of paper bags very simply. Each patient makes one puppet of herself and one of her perpetrator. The puppet that represents herself then confronts the perpetrator puppet.

*Masks* made by stapling two sheets of paper together, or more elaborate methods, are used as an exercise to help the survivor explore "what is on the outside that people see," and "what is on the inside." This helps to address misconceptions about how the patient comes across.

These exercises have been very useful in groups that I have directed. Therapists are encouraged to use and modify them.

Treatment of the inpatient survivor is often short term because insurance companies typically dictate shorter stays. As stated, patients are encouraged to recognize that this treatment is only the beginning. Prior to a patient's discharge from the group, a "survivor discharge plan" can be written in the group in which group members write words of encouragement for the patient being discharged and list survivor slips, useful telephone numbers, or any information that may help the survivor.

## ■ Integrating Survivor Issues With Other Treatment Issues

It is crucial to the recovery of the survivor that she be helped to integrate all treatment issues. This means that issues related to abuse are brought into family therapy, substance abuse treatment, individual therapy, and other specialized therapies, such as groups to address eating disorders.

Families are often resistant to exploring sexual abuse issues in family therapy. This is often because the patient's disclosure triggers memories of abuse from the parents' childhood. Parents who are unaware that their child was abused must accept both the abuse and that their son or daughter is no longer a virgin. Parents often feel intensely guilty for failing to protect their child. These feelings are complicated when the perpetrator is a family member or has a close relationship with the family.

As hospital stays become shorter, patients often do not have adequate time to process their disclosure of abuse before they must tell their parents so that mandatory reporting of the abuse can be processed. When mandatory reporting is not an issue, the therapist must assess when issues of abuse should be brought up in treatment.

Issues that often come up include "parent splitting," where the patient maintains that they can tell one parent but not the other. The therapist needs to take a stand that both parents must be informed and that maintaining secrecy has a role in perpetuating sexual abuse. Patients have to recognize that, at least in inpatient family therapy, they can take a baby step and let the parents know of the issues. As with survivor therapy, the patient and the family need to recognize that continued discussion of these issues will take place in outpatient family therapy.

Parents may refuse to believe that their child was abused, and the therapist will need to protect the patient. It is helpful to review with the family, in the patient's presence, why the therapist believes the patient. Parents may be so overwhelmed by the disclosures that they protect the patient with statements such as, "She doesn't want to talk about it now."

Reporting the abuse is often difficult for the parents and the therapist. The therapist may question if the agency receiving the report will do anything with the information, and the family is often anxious about what will happen. Whenever possible, the parents should report the abuse in the presence of the therapist, which offers support for the patient. Therapy should always conclude with a referral to outpatient family therapy.

When the perpetrator is a parent, the therapist should protect the patient by building an alliance with the nonoffending spouse and involving protective agencies and the police as soon as possible. Also, the perpetrator's involvement with the patient should be limited and monitored when possible.

The therapist must assess whether it is safe for the patient to return home and must make recommendations to the proper authorities. The perpetrator needs to be out of the home and kept away from the patient. This is a lot to accomplish in short hospitalizations.

Regarding issues of substance abuse, patients need to explore how substance abuse may have contributed to their abuse, or how they use alcohol or substance abuse to avoid thinking about their abuse. The abuse of drugs and alcohol often ties in to a pattern of risk-taking behavior. Issues related to substance abuse need to come up in survivor groups, and patients, to be survivors, need to make a commitment to sobriety and become deeply involved in support groups for alcohol/drugs.

Eating disorders are also prevalent in survivors. Issues related to needing to be in control, and controlling their outward appearance, need to be addressed. These control issues must be integrated with survivor issues and the patients' feelings about themselves sexually.

Finally, all survivors can benefit from individual therapy as well as group therapy. In hospitals, individual therapy is usually provided by the psychiatrist. The psychiatrist can help the patient explore how issues of abuse tie in to depression, suicidal behavior, self-destructive acts, and other issues. It is the individual therapist's job to integrate the patient's issues.

## ■ Conclusion

More and more psychiatric hospitals for adolescents are recognizing the importance of offering specialized treatment to survivors of sexual abuse. Sexual abuse treatment offers the survivor of sexual abuse a safe place to begin processing issues with, ideally, same-sex peers who have similar abuse issues. Hospitalized survivors must realize that they will not be "cured" of their survivor issues, but that they can begin the process of healing. Survivors can benefit from verbal and nonverbal therapies, and the therapist should use his or her own creative abilities when designing therapies. Survivor issues should be integrated with family therapy and individual therapy, and survivors should be helped to connect their sexual abuse issues with other significant problems such as substance abuse and eating disorder issues.

## Appendix A

# Personal Involvement and Socialization With Patients/Code of Ethics

**I. Policy**

To provide a consistent therapeutic approach to patient care, hospital staff shall not form social relationships with patients. Staff will have the responsibility to notify their supervisor immediately if they know a patient that is being admitted.

**II. Purpose**

To provide and maintain a therapeutic environment for patients through a professional, empathic, and objective approach to patient care and treatment.

**III. Procedure**

1. Hospital personnel shall not initiate social relationships with patients at any time during their hospitalization or after discharge under any circumstances. Social relationships will be defined as written letters, phone calls, or any other type of communication.

The unanticipated social contact that may arise through an employee's family member or friend shall not constitute a violation of this policy. If this should occur, the employee will not disclose any information regarding the hospitalization of the patient. This type of social contact will be reported to their supervisor.

2. Hospital personnel will not respond to any patient-initiated social relationships. Hospital personnel have the responsibility to report to their supervisor immediately if a patient has contacted or tried to contact them in any way. An incident report may be required.

3. Hospital personnel will notify their supervisor immediately if he/she has had any previous contact with a patient being admitted.

4. Hospital personnel shall only accompany patients off the hospital grounds in conjunction with the treatment plan, program activities, or physician's order and will adhere to the schedule of the activity.

5. Under no circumstances will hospital personnel accept money, tips, or gifts from patients or their families. Hospital personnel will not give patients gifts of any kind.

6. Abuse of this policy shall result in termination of employment.

7. All hospital staff are to read and sign the current form for this policy upon hire.

## ■ Employee Code of Ethics

All employees are expected to behave in a manner that is appropriate and sensitive to providing excellent patient care. Every hospital employee is expected to exercise good judgment when dealing with patients and their families. At all times, employees are expected to be courteous with patients, their families, and other staff members. The following are examples of areas of particular importance where employees have constant responsibility:

1. Staff members may be in a patient's room only with the door open.
2. Socialization or communication with patients or their family members outside of scheduled work hours is not permitted unless a preexisting relationship exists or as specified in policy regarding staff members' families.
3. Socialization with patients outside the hospital is not acceptable except in the course of group therapeutic outings.
4. Socialization with patients after they have been discharged from the hospital is not permitted.
5. Discussions regarding patients are not to be held in front of other patients or any person not privileged to that communication.
6. Problems of a patient are not to be discussed with another patient by the hospital staff members.

7. Patients are not to be named or discussed with any personal associates outside the hospital setting except for authorized professional activities.

8. Personal problems or concerns of staff members are not to be discussed with the patient group or any member of this group.

9. Counseling of the patient regarding personal problems or involvement of staff in therapeutic discussions with patients outside the realm dictated by the physician in care plan conferences is discouraged and unacceptable.

10. Staff may not give gifts to patients.

11. Staff may not accept monetary or valuable gifts from patients or their families.

12. Patients are to be dealt with equally and fairly and the selection of "favorites" is not beneficial to any of the patient group.

13. Employees are to bring questions and problems regarding any facet of their employment with the hospital to their department director.

Questions about the above areas, questions about the expectations of your job performance, or questions about the appropriateness of your behavior with patients should be directed to your supervisor immediately.

## Appendix B

# Sexual Abuse Assessment

### I. The Setting

Conduct interview in a neutral setting (an office), not the patient's room. Give the patient as much control as possible: "Do you want the door open or shut?" and so on.

### II. Introduction

Neutralize the stigma of assessment by explaining that "I talk to most patients about abuse."

### III. Establish Trust

Explain reporting requirements, that abuse needs to be reported to authorities, and that this may vary from situation to situation. This may make some patients delay disclosure, but allows the therapist to be truthful. (Use child protective agencies as a resource about reporting.)

### IV. Definitions/Discipline

Ask patient to define and give examples of physical, sexual, and emotional abuse. "Does any of this happen to you? Please explain."

Explore how patient is/was disciplined. Which caretakers disciplined and how? Ask if any caretakers were substance abusers. If discipline was physical, ask if it stopped and at what age. Don't be judgmental. Get specifics.

### V. The Family Child Care Providers

"Did anyone ever make you feel uncomfortable? Why?"

Ask about doors on the bedrooms/bathrooms. Do family members knock before entering rooms? respect boundaries? read diaries? and so on.

"What happens at night after you go to sleep? Do you know if anyone in your family was abused? If so, how?"

## VI. The Patient

"Have you ever been abused? Tell me about it." If abuse is identified, ask when it began and ended. Ask patient to be specific. If patient is too uncomfortable, inform patient that interview can continue at a later time. If abuse disclosed is in adolescence, ask about earlier abuse in childhood (be aware of patient's nonverbal communication). If patient appears overwhelmed, ask if patient would like to finish interview at a later date.

## VII. Impact on Current Life

"How has being abused affected your life?" Discuss relationships with peers. "How does the abuse affect you sexually?" Ask about patient's sexual development. Is patient a virgin? If not, what made patient decide to lose her virginity? Was this a good decision? Does current sexual behavior connect with abuse issues? Does patient use birth control? Why or why not? How many sexual partners? Has patient ever felt used in a relationship? If abuse was by a same-sex perpetrator, explore impact. "Did you ever feel this made you gay?"

## VIII. Related Issues

Look for issues related to dissociation: "Are there periods of time you forget?" Self-mutilation. Hurting herself. Fire-setting. Hurting animals. Regarding friendships: Same age? Mainly with older or younger peers? Regarding perpetration: "Do you ever think you could do to someone else what was done to you?"

## IX. Explain Therapy

Describe survivor groups. Explain integrating survivor issues with other issues.

# Ritual Abuse
## *Traumas and Treatment*

**Gayle M. Stroh**

There are numerous accounts throughout the world about occult worshipping (Kahaner, 1988; Kluft, 1989; Ryder, 1992; Sakheim & Devine, 1992; Smith & Pazder, 1980; Stroh, 1993; Wedge, 1988). This chapter will focus on satanism rather than other types of cults, some of which have many similarities to reports of satanic ritual abuse. Stories are escalating as survivors are coming forward to report incidences of horrendous torture; brutal killings; cannibalism; ritualized group raping of children; human and animal sacrificing; the drinking of blood, urine, and feces; and numerous other human atrocities that are an assault to our minds. Such accounts leave authorities, therapists, clergy, educators, police officers, and others either denying the existence of such occurrences or feeling insecure, frightened, and naive as to how to approach the problem.

AUTHOR'S NOTE: Portions of this chapter have been presented at various conferences throughout the country (see reference list). I would like to extend sincere appreciation to Lois Myler and Donald Wismer for their unyielding support and dedication. I would also like to thank David Lee and the staff at Holly Road Mental Health Center for their belief in me and in the program.

A suitable definition of ritual abuse has been given by Sakheim and Devine (1992) from the Los Angeles County Commission for Women:

> A brutal form of abuse of children, adolescents, and adults, consisting of physical, sexual, and psychological abuse, and involving the use of rituals. Ritual does not necessarily mean satanic. However, most survivors state that they were ritually abused as part of satanic worship for the purpose of indoctrinating them into satanic beliefs and practices. Ritual abuse rarely consists of a single episode. It usually involves repeated abuse over an extended period of time. (p. xii)

The term *ritual abuse* will be used to describe the most severe repetitive and systematized types of traumatic experiences. When faced with clients who are reporting such devastating horrors, we are forced to confront our own countertransferential conflicts, which will be challenged as we react to the gruesome material related by these clients.

It is my contention that there are no experts in the area of ritual abuse; however, there are many clinicians who have had numerous cases where survivors have reported extensive histories of satanic ritual abuse. There are far more questions than answers at this point as we all grapple to understand such reports with little concrete evidence to support such claims. The similarities between hundreds of cases that have been and are being reported are uncanny. Such stories cannot be entirely confabulated. Yet we must approach this issue with uncertainty as authorities continue to work toward a deeper understanding of this very controversial issue.

## ■ Introduction

There has never been a time in history when human sacrifice has *not* occurred, whether the killing was in the name of war, ethnic cleansing, or some religious god, deity, or belief. It is plausible that human sacrifice exists in the name of Satan as well.

Breiner (1990) extensively researched the histories of infanticide and human sacrifice. He compared five ancient cultures: Egyptian, Greek, Hebrew, Roman, and Chinese. His primary focus was on the roles that children and females played in each of the cultures, as well as the reasons behind massive slaughters that occurred, particularly of children. Breiner provides an excellent overview of the primitive rage and sadistic impulses inherent within the human species. With the massive amounts of violence that confront us daily via various media sources, it would seem absurd for us to deny the existence of ritualized abuse.

The Dissociative Disorder Program in central Michigan has been in existence since 1986 and is a partial hospitalization treatment center in which patients who are in the program attend from 9:00 a.m. until 3:00 p.m. This particular program was designed to accommodate the needs of individuals who had endured catastrophic traumatization throughout much of their childhood and who often use dissociation as a primary defense. After a 2-hour evaluation process, individuals are assigned to one of three existing groups that meets 2, 3, or 5 days per week.

During the early part of the year following the program's inception, one patient from each of the three groups began reporting experiences of ritual abuse. None of them knew of each other and they traveled long distances from opposite parts of the state. As the group therapists began describing similar stories from a patient in each of their groups, it became increasingly more difficult to deny that some type of ritual experiences had occurred. Since that time, approximately 100 similar types of reports have been made, although not all of the reports involved satanic ritual abuse. There were reports of similar types of torture that were claimed to have been connected with Christianity as well as with Native American rituals and those involving Jewish ceremonial rituals.

Over the past decade, particularly in the past few years, numerous books and articles have surfaced that consist of autobiographies; those who strongly disbelieve all of the reports that have been surfacing; those who adamantly profess that there is a mass conspiracy; and those somewhere in the middle who are grappling with this issue and are trying to understand what is truly "going on out there."

## ■ Case Studies

### Case 1

Jack was referred to the program in 1988 for treatment of his dissociative disorder. He was in his early 40s, married, and the father of four children ranging in age from 12 to 25 years. He had a long history of moving his family from state to state on an impulse. Jack had had numerous business ventures, but his need to constantly move created many failures because he would often leave prior to job completions.

Jack's symptoms at the time of his entrance into the treatment program involved frequent absences from the home during the night with no recall of where he had been; severe self-mutilation of the penis; the use of large dildos on himself until bleeding occurred; wearing women's clothing; a vengeance toward black males and men who belonged to motorcycle groups and wore black leather jackets; and exposing himself in public places after an attractive female had walked by. He timed the exposure so that he barely avoided being seen.

During the hundreds of hours of therapy that ensued, Jack began to have a greater awareness of an alternate part of himself, Jackie, who was responsible for his cross-dressing. Jackie would wear a red dress and heels in public and perceive that the strange looks "she" received had to do with "her" beauty. This part of Jack was blind to his very long beard and often was attracted to other males who cross-dressed as well.

Jack began to recall satanic ritual memories that involved repeated rapes by males. He attained a female persona as a means of managing the brutal rapes. He was no longer involved in cult activities after the age of 7; however, his behavior patterns frequently repeated the earlier traumas. The hatred toward black men and men wearing black leather jackets was attributed to men wearing black robes, one of whom was his father. Jack's need to mutilate his penis served to "castrate" those men whom he was helpless to stop from raping him. It also was an attempt to get rid of his identification as a man, which meant savagely harming others, and to please his mother, who repeatedly told him she wished he were a girl. This was part of the "home-based" training that he received in preparation for cult involvement.

After months of uncovering cult memories, Jack believed that a young woman in the cult who was his trainer was also his biological mother. This woman provided some semblance of nurturing and approval whenever he performed a ceremonial task well. Jack recalled that, at the age of 7, he walked toward an altar where he was forced to watch this mother being sacrificed. This event was the primary reason he dressed as a woman and wore red. He saw himself as the long-lost mother, and the red represented his wish to keep her alive, or bring her back to life. Wearing female clothing represented a perceived closeness to his cult mother as well as a way to remain "inside" of her as he wore "her" clothing. After Jack was able to fully grieve the loss of this woman, he was able to get rid of all of the clothing and has never cross-dressed again.

The bleeding from the rectum served as a repetition compulsion of the repeated rapes he had endured. In addition, the Jackie part of him perceived that she was indeed a woman who had menstrual cycles. Jack later learned that during his evening absences, he was prowling areas and places where prostitutes frequented. In particular, he was drawn to young black women, whom he would pick up. He then became terrified and needed to get rid of them, so he quickly dropped them off again. At other times, he frequented either bars with topless dancers or those that catered to transsexuals and cross-dressing males. During therapy, Jack learned that his cult mother had been of Native American heritage and wore a black robe, which accounted not only for his desire to pick up black women and the related fear of being sexual with them, but also for the terror associated with having them leave him, as in the memory of his cult mother. The need to frequent topless bars had to do with his need to find the mother that he had lost. He had always been drawn to women with large breasts; as a little boy he had been allowed to suckle repeatedly with his cult mother as well as other women. The females to whom he exposed himself were all dark in their features and were approximately the age that Jack perceived his mother to have been when she was killed.

This was a complex case in which Jack could not have overcome the destructive patterns of his behaviors had he not confronted the ritual abuse memories. Over the past 5½ years of intensive psychotherapy, Jack has confronted numerous cult memories and, as a result, no longer has dissociative episodes, nor does he engage in any of the self-destructive patterns that brought him into treatment.

## Case 2

Bonnie is a 43-year-old single woman who had an extensive hospitalization history prior to being evaluated for the partial hospitalization program in 1990. At that time, she reported a long-standing history of compulsive masturbation and exposing herself. Another problematic area concerned sleep patterns, whereby Bonnie would engage in compulsive behaviors all night long and sleep during the day. In addition, she was a compulsive overeater and an alcoholic. She had received treatment for her food and sexual addictions via specialized inpatient treatment centers, with unsuccessful results. She has not had a drink in

8 years and attends numerous 12-step programs. Bonnie was the second youngest of eight children raised in the Northwest by a prominent Catholic family. Her father was a well-respected businessman in the community. Her mother was a receptionist for the church. Bonnie and a sister 11 years older than she entered the convent at a young age; however, Bonnie left during her mid-20s due to guilt and shame over her sexual compulsions. Bonnie cared for both of her aging parents as they became increasingly ill. Her mother died in 1980 and her father in 1986. Neither she nor the sister who had been in the convent were included in their parents' wills. This has been a very painful issue for Bonnie because she perceived herself as her father's favored child.

During the time that Bonnie was in the program, she brought in art projects that involved drawings of large animals in attacking and threatening postures. Her art work frequently involved the bloodied corpses of animals and humans, and she had no idea why she created such pictures. Bonnie was in a group that did not have other ritual abuse survivors in it and, at that time, she had not been exposed to anyone else who had had such experiences. The responsibility of recalling memories was placed on her, and hypnosis was never done. Gradually, Bonnie began to recall ritualized sexual experiences that involved her father, as well as his involving her in child prostitution and pornography. Her father masturbated her as a means of training her to dissociate from other torturous acts that were being performed on or around her. She was suppose to focus all of her attention on sexual sensations so that she would not see or remember emotionally charged events that occurred simultaneously. The difficulty with remembering always involved intense sexual stimulation, on which Bonnie preferred to focus rather than the horrifying pain associated with observing or participating in sacrifices that were being performed.

Bonnie continues to have difficulty in the area of intimacy. She never felt that dating, let alone marriage, were ever an option for her. She believed that she was married to her father during a cult ritual; therefore, she saw herself as his. With women, Bonnie quickly formed strong, intense attachments. She reports that none of these relationships became sexualized. Whenever her female friend at the time moved away or became disinterested, Bonnie had severe separation anxiety and lapsed into a deep depression. This extreme reaction was related to a memory that Bonnie had where, at the age of 2, she was forced to watch and participate in the sacrifice of her cult mother. This memory involved what Bonnie felt had been the only nurturing she had ever gotten. At 2 years of age, Bonnie was handed over to her father for cult training after her perceived mother was sacrificed. Her father's intention was to force the vulnerable child to attach to him as a replacement for the lost mother. Bonnie had always considered her masturbation to be a means by which she "nurtured" herself; however, it has become clear that this compulsion served to maintain an attachment with her father as well as the mother who preceded him. In addition to the perceived comfort she attained through masturbation, the behavior also served to prevent memories from surfacing.

## ■ Fact or Fiction?

Hundreds, perhaps thousands, of reports of satanic cult rituals are occurring throughout much of the world (Breiner, 1990; Ewing, 1990; Kahaner, 1988; Richardson, Best, & Bromley, 1991; Ryder, 1992; Sakheim & Devine, 1992; Strean & Freeman, 1991; Stroh, 1993; Van Benschoten, 1990). Most of the survivors who are reporting ritual abuse histories are from the United States. It is possible that ritual abuse experiences are underreported or disbelieved in other countries of the world; it is also possible that such incidences are overreported and overly believed in America. The most likely truth resides somewhere in the middle.

For a moment, let us review the events of just 1 week in our history. On April 19, 1993, we saw the tragic end of a standoff between federal agents and the Branch Davidian cult members, and we asked ourselves, "How could this happen?"

On April 20, 1993, reports flooded the media of a 3-year-old boy from Chicago. Joey Wallace was conceived and delivered in a mental institute. His mother had spent much of 12 years in the institute for behaviors that were violent. She had a history of eating batteries, setting herself on fire, and violently attacking others. There was documentation that she stated she would kill her young son if she ever got him back. Yet, after her son had spent 3 years in foster care and had been placed in the care of a foster couple who were reportedly very loving, a judge granted custody to Joey's mother. Three weeks later he was found strangled by an electrical cord. His mother admitted to the killing. Again we have to ask ourselves, "How could this have happened?"

On April 23, 1993, the day Joey Wallace was buried, the first U.S. Holocaust Museum opened in Washington, DC. Protesters marched outside, shouting their disbelief that there had ever been a holocaust. At this we ask ourselves, "With all of the stories that survivors have told, with all of the evidence that exists, how can anyone disbelieve?" Ethnic cleansing persists in Bosnia and is known to exist in other countries to varying degrees as well. Again we are appalled at the prevalence of violence in our country and throughout the world.

Those who reside in a white-picket-fence, middle-class world may find it difficult to fathom such human atrocities. The prospect of people sacrificing humans and animals, torturing and ritually raping children, committing cannibalism, and drinking blood, urine, and feces is an assault to the mind. Not in our backyards can this be happening! Yet such reports flood the offices of clinicians, police officers, educators, clergymen, and so on, and we ask ourselves, "How can this be happening?" The very thought challenges our basic need for safety and security, for trust! How can this be possible? Because it has always been! This feels too close to home.

This is not to imply that all of the reports of ritual abuse are accurate or to be believed. In the years that I have worked with cases of ritual abuse, some individuals have retracted partial memories that did not fit into the history they had recalled. In addition, some clients have fabricated entire ritual abuse histories; this issue will be dealt with later in the chapter. However, for the most part, reports of ritual abuse experiences are incredibly similar in detail, which I have not as yet seen in writing. The intricacy of the details and relief of severe symptoms that had plagued these patients prior to the memory and resolution of cult events strongly suggest that there must be some validity to the reports of satanic ritual abuse that have been surfacing.

### ■ Types of Traumas

There are numerous theories that pertain to the reports of satanic ritual abuse. I will attempt to present a synopsis of approximately 100 ritual abuse cases that have been presented over the years at the partial hospitalization program as well as from my private practice.

During the early stages of treatment, most of the survivors, both male and female, recall instances of incest with a father or father figure. The next phase of memory retrieval has to do with recall of ritual abuse experiences. These traumas involve having to be buried in a coffin, grave, or hole with body parts of both animals and humans. In addition,

patients report that as young children, they had to witness and participate in animal and human sacrifices, which they were led to believe were
their fault. Other traumas involve ritual rapes, forced sexual involvement
with animals and other children, child pornography and child prostitution, as well as a ceremony that involves being born of the beast, Satan.

At a later age, children experience a wedding ceremony in which they
are "wed" to Satan. Drugs of all types are reportedly used while the
children are trained to use dissociative defenses. As young children,
they are not allowed to have friends unless the family provides them.
As a result, a child quickly formulates an attachment to the friend that
is provided. A relationship is allowed to develop, and then the child is
forced to kill his or her only friend, which strengthens the child's
attachment to the cult and to Satan, who is omnipresent. Patients report
extensive histories of cannibalism and drinking the blood of those who
have been sacrificed. As children, they are taught to make reality a
fantasy or bad dream. Survivors report programming, where they learn
all types of triggers for maintaining control over children. Such reports
occur in varying degrees as noted in the literature (Ryder, 1992; Sakheim
& Devine, 1992; Smith & Pazder, 1981; Wedge, 1988). One must use
caution when working with survivors of ritual abuse because many
clinicians have been known to expend all of their energy, over years of
therapy, focusing on programming and triggers while minimizing the
underlying traumas.

The final trauma that survivors report has to do with sexual abuse
experiences that involved their mothers or women who were considered to be their mothers. I collected data from approximately 150
individuals who were evaluated for the dissociative program. Results
overwhelmingly indicated that, for both male and female adult survivors, recollection of incest by a father or other male perpetrator as well
as incidences of ritual abuse always preceded memories of incest by a
mother or maternal figure. This phenomenon was addressed by Kasl
(1990) when she related a number of reasons that individuals were
fearful of discussing issues of abuse by a female perpetrator. In another
study, Mathews, Mathews, and Speltz (1990) focused on characteristics
of female offenders and provided an excellent overview of the levels of
sexual abuse in which females engage, as well as an analysis of the
motivational factors inherent in such offenses. It is my contention (Stroh,
1992) that there is a considerable cultural taboo against a mother's
incestuous relationship with her child, or any child, so that the young

recipient of such abuse has to either dissociate it or repress such awareness deep within the unconscious.

With regard to survivors of ritual abuse, many of them who report that they were born into a cult with intergenerational ties also share painful memories of having been attached to mother figures whom they perceived to be very nurturing. When the survivors reached the age of 2, the mother figures either became trainers who began to torture them or were brutally killed as the children were forced to watch and often participate. The whole ceremony appears to be connected to a particular ritual in which young children are officially "handed over" to become members of the cult "family." The 2- to 3-year-olds are set up to believe that they have done something terribly wrong and, as a result, the mother must become cruel, or must die. This process destroys the early attachment that had developed so that the cult commands control and becomes the object of the child's attachment.

As adults, this early attachment loss is often replicated in their relationships. They often search desperately for this early nurturing mother, although the memory of her has been dissociated and/or repressed from conscious awareness, as in the case of Jack. One of the most difficult aspects of their recovery is dealing with what was lost to them and will never return: the wished-for mother of yesteryear. These individuals tend to become easily frustrated in their relationships because their partners can never (and should not try to) live up to the survivors' perceptions of an idealistic mother. This also plays out in the therapy arena, which is the reason that very clear boundaries must be established and consistently upheld.

A part of the early training that survivors have reported is the repetition of messages that were given to them as children. There have been numerous accounts of this patterning, which is also associated with some type of painful reinforcement. As a result, behavioral modification techniques are employed that train young minds to respond as the perpetrators demand. Many have talked about electrical shock being used, as well as tape recordings that were used to force them to remain awake over an extended period of time. Other types of tortures were employed depending on the particular "teaching" that was necessary. As indicated earlier, the particular words, stories, and associated torture techniques would be used later as triggers to maintain complete control over the developing minds of the children. Some individuals have reported that regular children's stories and songs were juxtaposed, with different words substituted that would also be used as triggers, or posthypnotic suggestions.

The various techniques of torture were often associated with the learning of some type of lesson. Usually the lesson concerned the issue of not talking, or so the children were led to believe. The many pets that were killed, and the sacrificing of other children and adults, served as opportunities for trainers to tell their trainees that the sacrifices had to occur because the children had been about to tell what was occurring in the cult. The magical thinking of the children led them to believe that they must have had a thought about telling and therefore the omnipotent adults "knew."

Adult survivors, as well as stories from children, have mentioned being cut in locations that would go unnoticed, such as the bottoms of their feet. Therefore, any walking ensured that the child would remember the lesson taught. In addition, others have talked about arms or hips being dislocated, or being hung by their hands or feet for long periods of time. Some have reported being placed in small cages in which movement was limited to a crouch or lying in a fetal position; they were left there for long periods of time without food and forced to eat their own excrement. Survivors have also talked about being beaten and kicked by various members of the cult and then being defecated and urinated on by those same members. Any type of excruciating pain imaginable has been reported in one form or another by individuals who state that they had been born into a satanic cult. Those who have reported only adolescent involvement have focused on the drugs that were given to recruit them into the cult activities, where sexual acts were photographed and used as blackmail if the individual threatened to tell or leave. Gradually, these adolescents were introduced to animal sacrifice, which may or may not have led to human sacrifice as well.

With regard to multiple rapes of children, many survivors have described numerous examples of being prepared for rape by their assigned "teacher/trainer." The reports involved an adult or a young adult female who inserted various objects into a 2- or 3-year-old child's rectum, as well as the vagina, as a means of preparing him or her to be raped during an upcoming cult ceremony. In addition, most survivors have reported that much of the abuse at home also involved sexual abuse that, at the time, seemed unconnected to the cult activity. The initiation ceremony, when the child was 2 to 3 years of age, involved being raped by the cult master; therefore, the trainer was held responsible for how well the young child had been prepared for the ceremony.

From that point on, the child experienced numerous rapes; sometimes, a group of men would repeatedly rape a child throughout an evening.

It has been reported that the earliest training involved pets and/or young animals being tortured and ultimately killed. Children were told that the same would happen to them, or their loved ones, if they talked or did not perform in the way specified. This usually ensured compliance. Gradually, larger animals and babies were sacrificed as a punishment for something the trainer or master implied that a child had done. Survivors have reported that as young children, they were placed, naked, in a grave or pit with the bodily remains of their loved ones for long periods of time. They have also reported that children are forced to kill other humans by the time they reach the age of 4.

Various drugs are used on young children for a variety of purposes, depending on the particular ceremony in which they are involved. They are forced to eat parts of the body of an animal or human as a means of gaining power associated with the killing. Survivors have reported that children are forced to ingest eyeballs, which remain inside of them and "watch" what they are doing at all times. They are told that the consumption of the heart ensures that the victim resides within them and can somehow be reborn at a later date. According to many accounts of various survivors of satanic ritual abuse (Kahaner, 1988; Ryder, 1992; Sakheim & Devine, 1992; Stroh, 1993; and others), cannibalism occurs often, and all of those involved in the ceremony are expected to ingest the remains of the animal and/or human that was sacrificed.

> *The earlier and more severe the traumatization, the greater the pathology on the developing ego structure of the child.*

## ■ Developmental Impact

It has been well documented over the past decade that a high correlation exists between severe early childhood traumatization and the use of dissociation as a primary defense mechanism. The perpetrators of the abuse are typically the children's parents; therefore, the children feel unprotected and helpless, forcing them to develop their own defense structures, which simulate protection from others. When the abuse persists in an unpredictable and ongoing manner throughout the child's early life, a dissociative defense is often used to varying degrees. The earlier and more severe the traumatization, the greater the pathology on the developing ego structure of the child. Dissociation can be considered a defense that is superimposed, like that of paranoia, onto an underlying character disorder. Once the survivors are able to tolerate their memories and to manage in their lives without relying on the dissociative defense, an underlying character disorder will require continued work.

Most survivors of intergenerational satanic ritual abuse report very systematic methods of torture and abuse. All of those with whom I have had contact have shared a similar sequence of events that occurred at specific ages. The most difficult issue that any of them confronted was the loss of a mother or perceived mother figure after approximately 2 to 3 years of age. The children are nurtured and "loved" by women that most survivors believe are their biological mothers. These women are perceived as separate from the home mother and to have functioned in some specified role within the cult. Because the first couple of years are essential to the developing ego structure of the child, it appears as though the allotted time period of 2 to 3 years serves to provide a very basic emotional foundation. Those who head the highly organized cult groups allow this basic nurturing to take place between the mother and her identified cult baby. When the child becomes a toddler, issues of separation and abandonment take precedence. By that time, it has been predetermined that the child has had sufficient attachment needs met, and an abrupt removal of the child from his or her mother follows. A ceremony then takes place in which the young child is officially handed over to the cult for the purposes of membership and training.

All of the survivors indicate that the mother with whom they were raised at home was often cold and indifferent to them. This perpetuates the child's need to seek out someone who was lost to him or her at a very young age. Sometimes the biological mother is killed in front of the toddler, who is told that it is his or her fault. As a result of this abrupt separation, the child is expected to attach quickly to the cult as his or her new family.

Because abuse often takes place in the home, the child begins to adhere to the rules imposed on him or her by those who oversee cult activities. It is believed that the woman in the home in which the child is placed may be forced to sacrifice and/or give up her own child to raise another's. As a result, the home mother grows to resent the child placed in her care because he or she is a constant reminder of her own child. This hate relationship serves to maintain dependence on the cult as a whole rather than allow the formulation of small close attachments that can reduce the powerful hold that the cult leaders have over their members.

Survivors also report torturous brainwashing techniques that are employed to teach them to dissociate. As a result, the adults within the cult continue to have greater control over them because the children incorporate the dissociative defense style and are often unaware of many of their own experiences, especially those that relate to cult activities.

Attachment objects such as loved pets, friends, parental figures, and cherished items are used as mechanisms to continually train the young child. As indicated earlier, the child is allowed to formulate an attachment as a means of using the relationship against the child. All of the survivors with whom I have worked have shared stories of being provided with an attachment object only to have it repeatedly used in a sacrifice, during which the child is told that he or she had been bad in some way. As a result, these individuals grow up to have serious difficulties in relationships of any kind. Survivors often gravitate toward people who attempt to rescue them, and when the rescuers are unable to fulfill the survivors' ravenous appetites for infantile love, they leave. This creates a repetition of the survivors' original trauma, leaving them feeling abandoned and experiencing an intense hatred toward the lost loved object. As a result, ritual abuse survivors often seek a replacement object and/or reject any and all attempts toward a relationship.

Survivors thus have severe problems with intimacy. They fear either being consumed by another's neediness or devouring others with the intensity of their own insatiable appetites for love. The love that they experience toward others is often infantile in its development. Adult survivors often marry mates who have limited affective responses. Such spouses are emotionally impoverished and offset the overreactiveness of their survivor-spouses. Ritual abuse survivors continually attempt to get a reaction out of their partners, which is a reenactment of their earliest relationships with their parents. They often feel unloved and unimportant, as though they do not exist, which is how they experienced their childhoods. As children, the only way they felt valued was via some role that they were required to perform, which then becomes recreated in their adult relationships. Adult survivors are on an unconscious quest to find their lost mothers, who have become idealized over the years. When they find the mother-replacements, they either cling to the individual or create constant upheaval that will eventually lead to the end of the relationship. Survivors experience the situation as victims and as the aggressors who have the power to get rid of previous loved objects. This issue will be discussed in greater detail in the next section.

> *Survivors often repeat unconsciously patterns of their histories as a means of gaining some mastery over the original trauma.*

The developmental impact of catastrophic trauma on the developing ego structure of the child is astronomical. Every stage of development has severe deficiencies that make it difficult for the survivor of such atrocities to manage anything resembling intimacy.

## ■ Treatment

When working with individuals who have experienced severe traumatization during their early years, one defense mechanism that is often noted is repetition compulsion. Survivors often repeat, unconsciously, patterns of their histories as a means of gaining some mastery over the original trauma. An example is Jack, who wore a red dress in public. Although he had some awareness that he was cross-dressing, he was unaware of the original trauma, in which his mother was sacrificed and her white gown was covered in blood. At an unconscious level, Jack was attempting to keep his mother alive so that he did not have to lose her. Most repetitions are not so drastic, but any symptoms of a continued repetition should be explored as an individual's effort to repeat and be continuously victimized by some past experience that he or she is helpless to change.

Many individuals have difficulty experiencing feelings of helplessness. As a result, they "select" behavioral patterns in which they become helpless as a means of avoiding such feelings from some childhood experience in which one parent or both intentionally harmed them. The goal is to assist these individuals in developing insight into the origin of the trauma and in experiencing directly the associated feelings of helplessness and loss.

Many survivors of ritual abuse experiences have difficulty remembering and talking about the horrific memories that involved human sacrifice, cannibalism, and so on. As indicated earlier, they have been told as young children that they or their loved ones would die if they remembered or talked to anyone about their cult experiences. One method of treating this type of fear is allowing the client to draw what happened or to write the story in a journal. Using either method of obtaining information has proved valuable because it appeals to the concrete thinking of the survivor. Neither drawing nor writing is "talking."

These clients experience considerable anxiety when making decisions. Such conflict is often experienced as internal warfare. The dissociative defense serves to assist survivors, as young children, from having to confront external conflicts for which they have no other method of managing. The goal of the treatment is to have them experience both sides of a current conflict. An example is clients who feel that they will be killed if they talk about their history. Rather than focusing on the splitting phenomenon, the therapist should assist patients in recalling who threatened them when they were children that they were unable to confront. Memories involve external situations that the patients could not manage and therefore have internalized in a repetition fashion as a means of feeling some sense of power. If the conflicts continue to involve two parts of the self, then the helplessness of the original traumas is never experienced and remains unresolved.

## Confabulation

The issue of fabricated memories has come to the forefront with the advent of an organization that receives increasing publicity regarding the occurrence of false memories. The basic premise is that many of the memories that surface during psychotherapy are the result of some suggestion induced by the therapist. Unfortunately, there are such events that do occur, especially when working with clients who are highly prone to suggestion. It is my belief that such suggestion is unintentionally made by well-meaning clinicians. However, it is also my belief that most of the stories that survivors report have a good degree of authenticity. The reality is that there has been little concrete evidence, to date, to support the claims of ritual abuse that survivors make.

As we grapple with the issues related to ritual abuse reports, we must also consider the possibility of a partial or entire confabulated memory or memories. Clinicians who have worked with this patient population on a full-time basis over many years were initially unable to detect the fraudulent memories. I have worked with several individuals who have retracted reports of abuse, and during the course of their treatment in the program, they fabricated entire memories yet abreacted the "memory" as though it were real. Much later in their treatment, they retracted major memories that they had spent considerable time resolving. I do not mean to suggest that all reports should be given extreme scrutiny, but fabricated memories are a possibility that we must consider when listening to our clients.

Why would clients make up such atrocious histories? There are a number of good explanations. First, as clinicians, we tend to minimize the horrific impact of severe emotional deprivation and neglect on the developing ego structure of a young child. As a result, we may imply, unintentionally, that for a client to have been traumatized, he or she must have experienced horrendous physical, sexual, and/or ritual abuse. This poses a dilemma for those clients who have been deprived of the basic emotional connections needed to assure their sense of being loved and cared for. Clients may feel as though they have to create experiences that will elicit compassion and reassurance from their therapist, who deems such traumas to be more serious.

Second, many clients who report histories of catastrophic traumatization have often experienced extreme abuse and neglect during their preverbal stage of development. Trauma that occurs to an infant or toddler cannot be expressed in language. Their experience of an event often has to do with images, sounds, tactile stimulation, and olfactory sensations. It is my belief that adult survivors experience intense bodily sensations and are unable to recall many preverbal experiences because they had no language at the time with which to describe the events, especially if the events involved extreme neglect and deprivation. As a result, many survivors create an experience that fits some prevailing feeling and abreact the event accordingly.

Third, individuals who have experienced severe abuse throughout much of their early lives often rely on some form of dissociation as a way to manage each event. This defense style serves to protect the developing ego structure of the young child from threats of annihilation. Dissociation is a defense of self-deception in which reality becomes fantasy and the child's rich fantasy world, simultaneously, becomes reality. As the defense style becomes increasingly more sophisticated over the years, these individuals are able to make any fantasied experience real by quickly running it through their elaborate internal systems and reacting accordingly.

Fourth, which is closely related to the first reason that clients fabricate memories, is their phenomenal ability to anticipate what is unconsciously expected of them. They had to be hypervigilant as children and to differentiate the verbal and non-

*Clients who have experienced catastrophic traumatization are often more proficient at interpreting other people's unconscious needs.*

verbal cues from their environment so that they could be prepared. Clients who have experienced catastrophic traumatization throughout their childhood are often more proficient at interpreting other people's unconscious needs than are those people themselves. As a result, if clients perceive that their therapists have unmet and unresolved rescue fantasies, they will often comply and provide their therapists with very regressive behaviors. If they sense that their therapists have difficulty with anger, they will often be indirect with their angry feelings: They will take out their anger either on themselves, in a self-abusive manner, or on another person rather than chance abandonment by voicing their anger toward their therapist directly. Such clients have a severely diminished sense of self and must rely on their environment to dictate their immediate identity. These clients are similar to chameleons in that they can quickly manufacture a false self as a means of performing any role that is perceived to be needed at the time. It is easy for them to act out traumas as a means of supplying a need for their therapists and others.

The issue of traumatophilia concerns some clients' insatiable appetites to reproduce real and/or fabricated traumas (Beahrs, 1991; Stroh, 1992, 1993). The excitation of the experience can serve as an adrenalin rush that, via repeated reenactment of a trauma or pseudotrauma, can create an addiction for the client as well as the therapist. Both the client and the therapist can become entrenched in endless hours of reenactment as a means of avoiding underlying issues with which both are uncomfortable.

A fifth reason why individuals fabricate stories is malingering, whereby clients create false memories as a means of avoiding responsibility for their lives. When working with such individuals, the clinician may become bored and may have difficulty remaining connected to the material that such clients create. If the therapist's reaction is not a countertransferential issue, there is a good probability that the client is malingering.

A sixth and final explanation for confabulated memories concerns extremely poor ego boundaries on the part of some clients. When some patients are exposed to a group situation, or have contact with other patients in an inpatient unit, they have difficulty differentiating others' memories from their own. I do not advocate hypnosis as a means of retrieving traumatic memories; it is my belief that such an intervention places the control of memories within the power of the therapist, who reenacts childhood experiences in which adults controlled the patient's feelings. I have found that these clients will remember the traumas they were forced to endure when they are ready to tolerate the memories and associated feelings without relying on dissociative defenses as a means of "forgetting" what they are not ready to know.

## Other Treatment Issues

When working with individuals who are highly prone to regression, it is important to give them permission to explore early traumas; however, the memories that they recall are often distorted. Clients need to know that they can retract partial or complete memories that, after further exploration, may differ significantly from their initial perceptions. Clinicians often collude with their client's memories as if they were recalled precisely as the trauma occurred. In previous therapies, clients have reported that they felt as though they could not retract memories that were distorted when they initially began remembering. Many patients have expressed gratitude after being given permission to misrecall early events.

It is often difficult to tell when clients are confabulating memories. If we feel bored and detached from a client who is in the midst of abreacting memories, especially if our reactions continue over a number of similar enactments, I have found this to be a fairly accurate measure that the client may be fabricating memories. It is essential that the therapist confront possible countertransferential reactions prior to confronting the client. A clinician who reacts to a client's abreactive experiences by accepting that each trauma occurred as accurately as the client describes will miss the aforementioned clues and create a collusion between him- or herself and the client. In reality, we will never know what our clients were forced to endure because we were not there when events occurred.

We are forced to rely on symptoms that provide unconscious clues about the nature of our clients' early experiences. As they work through their traumas, we should note an improvement in the types of symptoms with which our clients came into treatment. If the symptoms persist, especially long after abreactive work has been occurring, then fabrication and malingering must be considered.

> *Clients survived by believing that if they were good enough, they would finally have a second chance at a childhood.*

The most difficult part of therapy is the grief work, which is essential. Clients survived by believing that if they were good enough, if they worked hard enough, if they got through their proverbial war, they would finally have a second chance at a childhood that included loving, nurturing parents. This fantasy must be confronted throughout therapy. Our clients can never retrieve what they have lost. They can never become a child again and receive all of the nurturing that they missed. When clinicians attempt to rescue clients from their horrific pasts, they keep their clients' hopes and dreams alive. Our patients must begin to grieve the loss of childhood and all of the rights that should have been available. This process should begin as these issues surface in the earliest phases of their treatment.

It is essential that clinicians establish clear boundaries and remain consistent in their enforcement of the established rules, especially during the early and middle phases of the client's therapy. It is through predictability that our clients can begin to feel safe and secure. As a result, their energies will be directed toward resolving the issues that brought them in, rather than engaging in defense styles as a means of avoiding inconsistencies.

Treatment emphasis should be directed toward the patient's needs and available resources. Intensive exploratory uncovering should be avoided if the patient lacks the ego strength or finances to endure long-term intensive psychotherapy. The client's current life must be as important in the therapeutic process as his or her past. Sometimes, too much emphasis is placed on the past and little or no attention is given to their present struggles. Interpretations are essential and can assist clients in understanding how their reactions to current situations are related to their histories. A balance between present and past experiences is necessary so that individuals can gain insight into current relationship problems that are often a reenactment of earlier relationships with their families. Emphasis should be on current relationships and personal goals when the client is feeling too overwhelmed and unable to manage the intensity of uncovering historical traumas.

When working with ritual abuse victims, there are traumas that are more traumatizing than others that need to be explored, abreacted (not reenacted), and grieved. There seem to be specific ceremonial rituals that are experienced by most survivors that occur at specific periods in their lives: the death or separation from the perceived birth mother, who was experienced as loving, that occurs at approximately age 2; an induction as a cult member, which seems to occur at approximately the same time, or shortly thereafter, when the child is handed over for training; a marriage to Satan at approximately age 6; and a first pregnancy around ages 9 to 11, as well as additional pregnancies at very specific ages. It is not necessary for clients to recall each and every ritual event because all events involve traumas similar to those previously addressed, and clients do not need to spend years of therapy exploring every one of them. As they grieve those tragedies that are essential to their lives, other similar ritual experiences will also be resolved. Much of their lives have been lost as a result of the traumas they experienced, and we must not allow their remaining lives to be lost as they explore and resolve their histories. It is vital that these clients develop an adult life outside of the therapeutic arena. When patients are allowed to explore each and every trauma they endured, we are doing them an injustice and, in essence, repeating their histories, in which their identities were an encapsulation of the traumas they experienced. It is essential that therapy involve the grieving and releasing of a life that defined their existence. They need encouragement to develop new lives that are separate from their pasts. It is difficult for these patients to learn about healthy relationships and the risks that are inherent in their attempts to do so. Survivors of ritual abuse experiences will often attempt to remain in their recollection of further ritual traumas as a means of avoiding the pain and difficulty associated with the development of mature relationships and a healthier lifestyle. This is one of the most important tasks of our clinical work: teaching our clients to experience mature love.

## ■ Countertransference

When faced with patients who are reporting the experience of satanic ritual abuse, we are forced to confront our own countertransferential conflicts, which will be challenged as we react to the gruesome material related by these clients. It is vital that we examine the sadistic impulses and homicidal rage inherent in us all. Our beliefs regarding and reactions to our client's accounts are directly related to our own unresolved conflicts, which include sadistic and homicidal wishes (Stroh, 1991a).

Whether we do or do not accept these clients into our practices, our decisions will ultimately be based, in part, on our own unconscious, primitive needs. If we deny our feelings, we will communicate our apprehension to our clients in a variety of ways. Examples of our apprehensions include redirecting the client to topics that are less threatening to us, experiencing intense restlessness or sleepiness during sessions in which clients are describing cult rituals, being late or canceling sessions, and voicing disbelief to the client about the occurrence of satanic cults.

Clinicians may also invite such patients into their practices based on unmet rescue fantasies of their own, as well as unresolved conflicts that may include sadistic impulses. We often get into the clinical profession as a means of fixing our own family of origin. If therapists have not worked through their unconscious wishes to change or to be rescued from their persecutors of the past, such wishes will be transferred onto clients. A clinician may express an intense desire to rescue patients who have experienced catastrophic traumatizations throughout their childhood. As a result, these needy patients will intuitively sense the needs of their therapist and react accordingly. Ritually abused clients have shared their frustrations pertaining to this dilemma. On one hand, they want to please the therapist in the hope of being loved, and thus rescued. However, these clients also house resentment toward a therapist who unintentionally encourages helplessness and regression.

Many clinicians have voiced their wish to become experts in the area of ritual abuse and have surrounded themselves exclusively with clients who have reported ritual experiences. I have to wonder why anyone would want to spend all of his or her time treating this particular patient population. Perhaps the answer lies within some therapists' unresolved histories where rescue fantasies were unmet and the related unconscious, sadistic impulses and homicidal rage prevail. Such conflicts can be defended through an excessive need to rescue others. Ritual abuse survivors provide an excellent avenue for acting out others' unresolved rage. These clients often spend countless hours describing horrific ways in which they and others have been tortured and/or sacrificed. These patients have acted out their murderous rage, which most of us have been fearful of confronting within ourselves. When clinicians deny such impulses and urges within themselves, they may be relying unconsciously on the sadistic actions of their clients as a means of ridding themselves of similar, unresolved conflicts.

If therapists are experiencing difficulties with clients who have been ritually abused, and similar problematic patterns continue to arise with these particular clients, it is essential that therapists seek their own psychotherapy with a well-qualified clinician as a means of resolving conflicts that may be interfering in their work with these difficult clients. If such conflicts are not directly confronted outside of the therapeutic arena, we can unintentionally force our clients to act out such conflicts, thus reenacting their early traumatic histories. If we cannot accept our own "beast within," our efforts to help clients confront their beasts will fail (Stroh, 1991a).

When working with their first abuse clients, who often have a dissociative defense style, therapists often find themselves intrigued by their clients' complexity and the flamboyant behavior that they exhibit. Clinicians often become entrenched in the uniqueness of the defense styles and awed by the number and array of the various "personality" states within the patients. It is easy to become encapsulated by the patients' extensively traumatized pasts and overwhelming despair. Many clinicians become seduced by these phenomena and allow themselves to be taken in by the clients' perceptions of reality and their expectations of the therapists. Thus, when faced with a client diagnosed with a dissociative disorder, therapists abandon their theoretical stances and traditional therapeutic interventions and adapt to patients' implicit demands (Stroh, 1992).

Clients who have experienced ritual abuse histories force us to confront our rescue fantasies directly when they behave in a regressed state often portrayed as a terrified young child "alter." At such times, it is easier to believe that this is a young child rather than an adult who has regressed. We cannot rescue our patients from their torturous pasts, nor can we relieve them of their pain by relinquishing boundaries or reacting to them any differently than we would treat patients who are not diagnosed with a dissociative disorder.

Patients diagnosed with dissociative disorders will often convince their therapists that the therapist must behave in gratifying ways that challenge therapeutic boundaries. Clinicians often feel an obligation to gratify their clients' needs based on primitive identification needs of the therapists, in which they wanted someone to rescue them. The difficulty that arises is these clients' insatiable appetites for gratification. They unconsciously expect their therapists to meet many of the needs they missed as very young children: for us to become the ideal, all-loving parents whom they lost. Many of these patients, who have experienced profound traumas, expect their therapists to be available to them 24 hours a day. In addition, they seek specialized treatment that other clients do not receive. Examples include unlimited phone contacts beyond work hours; extended sessions; reenactment of traumas rather than abreactions (Stroh, 1992); and expectations that regressed "parts" should be treated accordingly, such as by rocking or holding them. When therapists are constantly gratifying early needs, they convey to their clients a distorted message about reality, and their patients will remain in regressed states for longer durations and create additional "needy child alters" in reaction to their therapists' countertransferential needs to nurture them. As a result, therapy is prolonged, dissociation encouraged, and traumas constantly reenacted rather than resolved (Stroh, 1991b). As previously noted, this serves to avoid the central issue related to the essential grief work. These patients need to grieve the early loss of what they can never regain: a childhood with nurturing parents.

Therapists have often verbalized their frustrations and feelings of helplessness when confronted with patients' hostility which is often manifested as "angry alters." It is essential to confront the transferential issues as therapists begin to realize their frustrations because such feelings are usually emotions projected by the patients, who felt helpless against their parents' rage. Often, the impulse of therapists is to identify with the helplessness. This reaction perpetuates the emergence of hostile behaviors by switching to other alter states, where individuals simultaneously experience resentment for being perceived as children.

With regard to issues of seduction and anger, many clinicians have reported that they have developed preferences for alter states who are seductive and who use sexuality as a means of gaining acceptance and approval from their therapists. Because all clients who have experienced ritual abuse histories have been sexually abused and ritually raped on numerous occasions by many adults, they learned that the only way to manage their rage at being victimized was to pretend that they enjoyed the act. For most of these patients, this became the only sense of closeness that they experienced. They learned to respond to adults in this manner because it was the only means by which they felt valued. The intensity of their rage surrounds the reality that they were being used and discarded rather than truly loved.

When therapists act on their own unresolved need to be loved by encouraging their patients to behave in a seductive manner, many of these patients will comply as a means of gaining approval. Many clients have reported incidences of sexual involvement with their therapists. I am aware of several successful lawsuits against former therapists, both male and female, who became sexually involved with clients who had a dissociative disorder. As a result, unresolved Oedipal issues resurfaced and the regressed patients reexperienced the incestuous relationship of their childhood. They associate sex with love and will comply with the therapists' wishes for love as a means of feeling loved themselves. However, feelings of intense anger will emerge as well because the client reexperiences the feelings of being used and having to "feed" the parent-object once again, rather than being the recipient of the "feeding" experience. The rage will be either acted out within the context of the therapy hour or displaced onto others after leaving the office.

Patients who have endured catastrophic traumatization throughout much of their early lives are experts at interpreting the needs and expectations of those around them and have developed extraordinary ways of meeting the needs of others as a means of gaining acceptance and approval. The most likely response is one of compliance; the client perceives that the therapist is uncomfortable with certain feelings, and thus avoids them. Such feelings, which belong in the therapy arena, will surface in the client's interpersonal relationships as a means of protecting the therapist. One patient reported that she could always tell when her therapist needed a break from her and, as a result, would comply by announcing that she was suicidal, prompting her therapist to put her in the hospital for a couple of weeks. We, as therapists, may perceive patients' compliance as gratifying and as evidence of their trust in us. It is often our own narcissistic investment that prevents us from interpreting their needs and exploring the underlying dynamics that the patient experiences but does not express for fear of rejection and abandonment. As a result, the patient often continues to engage in such behavior patterns as a resistance to confronting dissociated behaviors of alters, who express anger or other disowned and unacceptable feelings. These feelings may or may not be directed at the therapist, who prefers compliance (as did everyone else in the client's childhood).

These patients share the most horrifying histories imaginable. Many of them enter therapy with little or no recall of their ritual abuse. Too often, unbeknownst to the therapists, they are still actively involved in their cult families and related practices. If clinicians and other helping professionals are aware of patients' current involvement in cults, such involvement poses ethical and moral dilemmas.

The therapeutic process is often slow and arduous for clients and therapists alike. It is recommended that no one work with these patients without good supervision and support. In addition, therapists must have a well-balanced and satisfactory life outside of their practices. That is where the emotional refueling comes from, so that we can continue to work with the devastating traumas these patients have been forced to endure. It is not acceptable to use clients as a means of getting all of our needs met. It confuses the clients, who comply with our needs and respond accordingly.

## ■ Conclusion

This chapter has attempted to provide a brief overview of the difficult issues that arise when therapists are confronted with clients who have experienced extensive histories of ritual abuse. It is absolutely essential that we learn as much as we can as we grapple with the dilemmas and the moral and ethical issues inherent in working with this very difficult and complex patient population. It will take considerable time, patience, and concrete evidence before we can fully comprehend the ritual abuse histories that are being reported all over the world.

I have found it invaluable to have considerable knowledge of the developmental issues that children of differing ages face as a result of severe traumatization. In addition, it is strongly recommended that therapists seek supervision from authorities in the field who have experience working with clients who have endured catastrophic traumatization. When working with survivors of any type of ritual abuse, therapists will be forced to confront their own unresolved childhood issues. If particular patterns continually occur in the therapeutic arena that create intense reactions within therapists, they might find it useful to seek individual psychotherapy as a means of confronting the countertransferential issues that surface.

Issues related to confabulation of memories must also be considered when working with patients who are very needy and who will do whatever is necessary as a means of feeling valued and loved. It is helpful to give clients permission to be confused about the memories that begin surfacing. Many clients will be grateful and feel less pressure to have accurate memories if less emphasis is placed on precise retrieval of experiences that occurred during overwhelming circumstances and at a very early age. It is essential that therapists "unplug from the drama, and work with the trauma!"

As stated earlier, there has never been a time in history when human sacrifice has *not* occurred, whether the killing was in the name of war, ethnic cleansing, or some religious god, deity, or belief. It is plausible that there has been human sacrifice, among other things, in the name of Satan as well. It is my contention that some children are, and have always been, sacrificed, tortured, and forced to perform human atrocities at the hands of "family" members. It will take years before concrete evidence emerges. I believe that even one child who has to endure such horrific experiences is one child too many.

# PART TWO

# Child Perpetrators

# 4

# Sexually Aggressive Children and Societal Response

## Hendrika B. Cantwell

There are many questions concerning children who are "sexually acting out" or are sexually aggressive toward younger, smaller, less powerful children. To begin with, terminology is far from settled. Although originally referred to as "child perpetrators" (Johnson, 1988), this appellation, borrowed from adults, now seems too stigmatizing. Terms such as "abuse reactive," "victim-perpetrators," and "trauma reactive" all imply that perpetrators have also been victims. It is well documented, however, that children who are sexually aggressive toward others beginning in late childhood and early adolescence are not necessarily victims of sexual abuse. The terms are incomplete if, by implication, they refer only to the previously sexually victimized. The appellation "prepubescent offenders" does not apply to the 4- to 7-year-olds who may not be "offending" in the adult sense (Johnson, 1991a, 1991b).

Terms need to be defined and agreed on. "Molestation," in its primary definition of "to meddle with, to annoy," is not a specifically sexual term. "Sexually intrusive" implies physical intrusion into an

AUTHOR'S NOTE: The author wishes to acknowledge with gratitude the editorial assistance of Christopher Cantwell.

orifice, which need not occur for behavior to be considered sexually aggressive. Thus in this chapter, the term "sexually aggressive" will be used.

Beyond this, there is little agreement as to what is normal, normative, abnormal, pathological, or aggressive when discussing children. No one knows what normal is. Adult predetermination of child sexual behavior is one possible standard, but more likely, "normal" depends on what is tolerated in the classroom, the playground, the neighborhood, or the house. Some behaviors that may be only exploratory, such as a child under 4 or 5 years old who puts a finger in another child's anus, may cause a great uproar among some adults. Although the child needs to be corrected and told that such behavior is socially unacceptable, the behavior itself is not necessarily sexual.

Childhood sexuality is not well tolerated by adults. Adults wish for sexual innocence in childhood in spite of the obvious evidence (erections, masturbation) that children are born with sexuality. This wishful thinking has manifested itself in ignoring childhood sexual aggression, as well as normal sexual development, rather than taking care to evaluate the potential harm one child may be causing another. Our aim must be to protect children from sexual aggression whether the aggressor be a young child or an adult. Although they are born with a sexual capacity, children's expression of it is culturally determined.

> *Although they are born with a sexual capacity, children's expression of it is culturally determined.*

Throughout modern history, knowledge and misinformation have stood side by side regarding sex and sexuality in childhood. I will discuss a few issues of the past, the knowledge more recently acquired, and some possible paths for the future. Sexual abuse of children is not a *newly* discovered phenomenon.

## ■ Some Historical Information

Today, most helping professions view child sexual abuse as something bad that is to be avoided, something that causes its victims long-term and wide-range suffering. This suffering includes, but is not limited to, substance abuse; sexual difficulties; depression; posttraumatic stress; dissociative disorders; the perpetuation of abuse into a new generation; and pain, terror, and dehumanization. Child abuse has been widespread and common for a long time. How society has regarded that evidence is what has been at variation. It has varied widely because of social, political, and historical forces at work through this period (Olafson, Corwin, & Summit, 1993). In all likelihood, societal regard for the issues discussed here will continue to change due to the same forces, so that what is generally seen and agreed on today may seem quite absurd 100 years from now. An example of a change taking place is the current argument and debate about the veracity of late memories reported by adults and children.

Simpson (1988) reports that as far back as the mid-18th century, 25% of capital rape cases in England involved children under 10 years old. A Parisian police commissioner in 1839 devoted a full page of his annual report to the sexual abuse of children (Tardieu, 1873). In Germany, there were 3,085 convictions for sex offenses against children in 1897, and 41,378 in 1904 (Moll, 1913). Apparently, the myth that sex with a child could cure venereal disease was widely acted on during that time. The Children's Home in Leytonstone, England was founded in 1865 for girls under 12 years old, including some as young as 6, "who had been so grievously dragged into terrible sins that they could no longer be kept in the village school nor in the orphan homes" (Cotton, 1873, as quoted by Olafson et al., 1993). An effort to "treat" them was made. Today, we also place such children in residential care facilities (RCCF) as a result of our cognate inability to accommodate them in schools or communities.

In the mid-19th century, French physicians examined tens of thousands of cases of child sexual abuse and rape in order to document the great frequency of sexual assaults against children and to verify that such attacks were truthfully reported by the children. They further argued that fathers and brothers were often the perpetrators and that "higher education" did nothing to prevent men from committing such acts (Olafson et al., 1993). Early in his career, Freud understood that incest existed among his female patients, including those from respectable families, and also that the greater frequency of hysteria in women stemmed from the fact that they were sexually assaulted more frequently than were boys (Olafson et al., 1993).

Although child-adult sexual interaction has been widely reported since the 19th century, there has also been a consistent tendency toward the minimization of these incidents. Prosecution of offenders often has been seen as victimization of adult males, rather than as protection of children involved in child-adult sexual interactions. According to the

Oedipal complex, children should be blamed for wishful thinking and fantasizing about sexual interaction with the parent of the opposite sex.

During the 1940s, a common view labeled a child a "participating victim" or a "sex delinquent" who was assessed responsibility for seducing an adult. Sexual modernists such as Kinsey viewed the fondling of a child's genitals by an adult with a certain optimism and permissivity, suggesting that the most traumatic aspect of the experience might be in the alarm sounded by other adults or police. Members of Kinsey's team also suggested affable analogues in the animal kingdom.

Mother-based etiologies also have been common in this century in which parental seductiveness, especially female, could be assigned blame. In sum, these 20th-century redefinitions blurred the issues by "degendering" perpetrators, locating most sexual abuse outside the respectable family, criminalizing its young victims, and pathologizing child abuse crusaders by labeling them sexually abnormal. (See Olafson et al., 1993, for a detailed exploration of the historical background of child sexual abuse.) It remains to be seen whether the present concern for poor mental health arising from sexual exploitation will remain at the forefront of societal policies or whether the knowledge will once again be suppressed (Summit, 1988).

## ■ Beginning Considerations

The question that needs to be asked in our discussion is, By what standards are we to regard children's actions? Obviously, words like "normal" and "adult" are societally determined, and children by their very definition are in the process of learning about and growing into such roles vis-à-vis that society. William Friedrich's (1993) recent description of the frequency with which some specific sexual behaviors of children were witnessed by parents who responded to his questionnaire is particularly revealing. Some behaviors reported were the ordinary things that children do, whereas other behaviors were more overtly sexual and probably not normal. The latter were rare, and the former, frequent (Friedrich et al., 1992). The behaviors varied in frequency with age, as expected, and were related to child development. Overtly sexual behaviors are more common among little children and disappear as they get older, whereas others, such as a sexualized pretending with Ken and Barbie dolls, might occur in school-aged children. It provides us with a sense of how we might regard children's actions.

Discerning the normality or abnormality of a behavior may not be as important as determining whether an imbalance of power between two children places one of them at the mercy of the other. If so, the behavior may be compared to that of adult sexual perpetrators, who always operate from an unequal power base. Even if two youngsters appear to be about the same size and age, they do not necessarily share equal power (Isaacs, 1992). One child may occupy a position of power because of greater popularity or leadership of the athletic crowd.

> *It must be determined whether an imbalance of power between two children places one of them at the mercy of the other.*

Care must be taken to differentiate consent from compliance or acquiescence. The less powerful child, who has no idea of the consequences of the proposed behavior, is asked for consent, which clearly cannot be given. There may be punishment associated with what is proposed. A child may say, "(S)he liked it and agreed to it and wanted me to do it." Such statements are common from adult as well as young perpetrators. The tactic may be to convince a child victim to cooperate, but caution should be taken when drawing conclusions: Some who appear to be victims are engaging others to perform and teaching acts that were previously done to them by someone else.

In the investigation of young sexual abuse perpetrators, a major concern is that these children, especially those under 7 years old, are almost always victims themselves of sexual abuse (Garland & Dougher, 1990; Gil & Johnson, 1993; Johnson, 1988, 1989a). Children replay what has been modeled for them, either by an adult or another child. Sometimes an inquiry becomes very muddled because many children are involved in imitating each other's behavior, so that no source for the behavior is found. That source usually is an adult or adolescent who initiated one of the children, who then passed it on as a fun game to play (Cantwell, 1988).

Investigators have come to realize that perpetrators are quite numerous among younger age groups (Feldman et al., 1991). Therapists, working with adults, realize that their patients often begin perpetrating in adolescence. Those involved therapeutically with teenagers find that many begin their sexual aggression in earlier childhood. Perpetrators who are 7 years old or younger are not uncommon. Combining that knowledge with the concern about young perpetrators of sexual abuse has increased our willingness to recognize that their assaultive behavior may not be harmless, nor just childish experimentation, and may have far-reaching consequences (Friedrich, Beilke, & Urquiza, 1988; Gale, Thompson, Moran, & Sack, 1988; Miau, 1986; Reinhart, 1987).

In the 1980s, a new outcry began against the victimization of children. The interest was reflected in an increase of books, articles, and studies, as well as print, radio, and television coverage. In the past 10 years, child sexual abuse has received particular attention. As might be expected, there are professional debates regarding the truthfulness of children and how best to determine the following: whether children are lying (Faller, 1984, 1988; Jones & McQuiston, 1987); the alleged fabrication of sexual abuse complaints in custody disputes (Thoennes & Tjaden, 1990); the suggestibility of children and who is able to influence them (Ceci, Ross, & Toglia, 1985; Cohen & Harnick, 1980); the significance of physical findings and the criminal process (Johnson, 1989a, 1991a, 1991b; Johnson & Berry, 1989); the need for child testimony (Goodman & Helgeson, 1988); whether testimony by a child is harmful or beneficial (Goodman & Jones, 1987); how children must be evaluated (Smolensky & Goodman, 1987); what evaluation of perpetrators shows (McGrath, 1990); whether there are recognizable patterns of profiles for perpetrators and victims (Becker & Quinsey, 1993; Berliner & Conte, 1993); and so on. The forceful expressions of opinion on both sides have been felt in a "backlash" (Coleman, 1989; Franklin, 1990) in the media as well as in public perceptions and influence on public policy.

Meanwhile, a need to treat adult and child victims of sexual abuse continues in spite of fewer dollars with which to do so. Instead, available funding appears destined for the expensive, elaborate, and adversarial environment of the criminal/civil court system.

Where, then, are the resources to help the children who, after being victimized, are now perpetrating and causing a new kind of havoc? They are both problems and victims. For example, the parents of victimized children are suing school districts when they can show that the schools knew other children to be perpetrators, and thus potential threats. Yet a school lacks the power to insist that a child and his or her parents receive therapy because of sexual misbehavior. Correspondingly, Child Protective Services (CPS) has no power to insist on therapy unless the case is heard in court and a court order for treatment is issued from a juvenile (civil), not criminal, court action.

Also, in practically every jurisdiction, judges are overwhelmed with other cases and are not eager to hear about a young child "playing at or being curious about sex," which is how most adults regard the problem of very young sexual aggressors. Few people understand that the victims are traumatized (Grosz, Kelly, Haase, & Kempe, 1992) and that some of the perpetrators are seriously and secretly preoccupied with and addicted to victimizing (Johnson, 1991b).

Although we give lip service in society to the concept that we want the best for *all* of our children, we do not provide adequate medical care, protection, supervision, education, guidance, or treatment (Hewlett, 1991). It is not surprising that elementary school children under 10 years of age who are seriously misbehaving (sexually or otherwise) are given inadequate, inappropriate, or no remedial attention, even though it is evident that to intervene in the present could save money and misery later. No one insists that the children receive help for their problems. When they turn 10, 11, or 12 years of age, depending on the jurisdiction, the same children can be charged criminally for behavior that, at a younger age, was simply not acted on. Having grown into adolescence or adulthood, their secretive skills have grown along with them, causing more trouble and proficiently creating more victims. Taxpayers bear a heavy burden for cases heard in court and subsequent supervision or incarceration to prevent perpetrators from harming others. If documented and publicized, the cost alone might be a good motivator to provide treatment for young, sexually aggressive children.

## ■ Sexual Exposure

"Of what avail our belief in free will? For her we were sleepwalkers caught in the current of an irresistible sexuality" (Durrell, 1978).

In spite of our supposed collective concern for our children's welfare, pornographic and sexually explicit material in conjunction with violence, death, and torture is omnipresent in all of our daily lives. Its availability and intrusive prevalence conveys to susceptible individuals, such as children, the idea that what they see adults do in television shows and films, in public, and in magazines and books must be acceptable. Perpetrators, in grooming children for later sexual activities, show them sexually explicit material to get cooperation. They show them pictures of other children apparently happy to be performing sexual acts. Cooperation becomes acceptable, especially with an offered reward. Medved (1992) made the point in his recent book that the film and television productions coming out of Hollywood are creating many of the problems in children that then must be dealt with by parents, schools, and, ultimately, society.

In talking with children about what they have seen and then done, they confirm that there is an element of "seeing is believing." Having fallen into a perpetrator's trap (usually a trusted adult) or having discovered their parents' pornographic videocassettes and imitated their contents, children are influenced to think that if their parents behave like that, it's all right for them to do it, too. However, they may also have a suspicion that it is not approved behavior, especially because the videocassette is usually hidden.

Clearly, if children are immersed in sexual images, their perceptions of wrongdoing by a perpetrator are severely blunted. Nevertheless, in the vocabulary of prevention strategies for the benefit of children, very little has been mentioned regarding the conflict between our society's repugnance for censorship and its desire to protect children. The voluntary discontinuance by parents of offending television channels, magazines, and videos is an eloquent accumulation of evidence that might be more universally noted. In truth, however, many adults do not want to be deprived of their right to such entertainment.

Consider also that many young children are home alone or with siblings. Television is their baby-sitter. When alone, they choose, and often have free access to, any program on any channel. Critics of television programming are told that parents can just turn off their televisions. "Just say no" is a poor response because children are often in charge of viewing. This is especially so during the daytime and early evening hours. In addition, there can be no possible preparation for or anticipation of inappropriate advertising that is sporadically interjected into innocent, harmless, and widely sanctioned family shows.

In some households, shared nudity is upheld as a good practice in child rearing, whereas in others, allowing children to watch parents having sexual intercourse is an accepted pattern. The child who comes to another child wanting to do what was observed at home or on television does not necessarily perceive this as inappropriate. Thus there may be a wide range of questions to be considered before one can know that a child is behaving pathologically. Imitation of adults is how children learn: A child who has never baked cookies at home would not suggest such an activity. Similarly, it is unlikely that a child not exposed to sexual activity would suggest doing it.

## ■ Child Sexual Abuse

Many who have been struggling with child maltreatment in all its manifestations in the past 3 decades have been disheartened in the past 10 years at all of the specialized interest, research, and conferences concerning sexual abuse. In fact, relatively less attention is paid to neglect or to verbal and emotional mistreatment, yet these account for as much of the damage to abused children in general as sexual misbehavior.

Child sexual abuse is classified as a criminal offense and this fact has helped to foster increased knowledge on both sides of a criminal proceeding. Court testimony predominantly concerns itself with the sexual matter because that is the possible criminal offense properly before the court. Issues involving the child's relationship to the parents and the parents' attitude and acceptance of the child have been shown to be of great importance in an adult's life outcome of childhood victimization (Beitchman et al., 1992).

On the other hand, neglect statistically accounts for more deaths among children. Nevertheless, there are few rules and little societal agreement about what is acceptable concerning parental supervision, even though the lack of it is a frequent culprit in neglect deaths, whether by guns, fire, or bathtub drownings.

Without adequate supervision, children who are frequently home alone may spend a lot of time looking at inappropriately violent television (Medved, 1992). They report being lonely and afraid, they may use drugs and alcohol, and they may be susceptible to exploitation by someone older (Berman, Winkleby, Chesterman, & Boyce, 1992; Dwyer, Danley, Sussman, & Johnson, 1990; Kelly et al., 1986; Richardson, McGuigan, Johnson, & Brannon, 1989; Zylke, 1988).

Parents often choose convenient and inexpensive supervision by another child. Although being a teenaged mother is not considered a good choice, a lot of child rearing (baby-sitting) is performed by children between 10 and 16 years of age. Margolin and Craft (1990) found that the youngest group, from 11 to 13 years old, was the most abusive toward its charges.

When a foreign name is attached to the activity, as in "au pair," wherein an adolescent from Europe comes to live with a family and look after the children while both parents are away from home for long hours, it suddenly has a glamour attached to it. Little is known about these young people: they are not educated in child care, and they may have come for the primary purpose of improving their English language skills or simply being in the United States. Child care competence or interest may be low.

Although poor-quality child supervision is not the exclusive province of young baby-sitters, about one third of the adults who were child sexual abuse victims report that they were victimized by older children, cousins, or siblings who were their baby-sitters (Margolin, 1991). These caretakers spanked, hit, slapped, beat, or sexually abused children to various degrees. In most families, parents believe that physical punishment is necessary, arguing that it is legal, that everybody does it, or that it was good for them when they were children. If older siblings were punished physically, they will pass it on to the younger ones when they get a chance to be in charge.

Sexual interaction between an older sibling and younger ones who are in his or her charge may similarly indicate past experience with parents. In a sexualized family environment, there may be a resulting preoccupation with sex or a need to dominate; either of these may result in sexual interaction (Green, 1984; Laviola, 1992). In other cases, curiosity seems to be the motivator. Usually, curious children are less threatening and less intrusive in their activity.

Neglected sibling groups sometimes become sexually interactive. Because neglectful households suffer from chaotic, unstructured conditions in which, for instance, children have no place to sleep, no belongings are personal, and boundaries of privacy are blurred, sexual boundaries are easily blurred as well. Considering the paucity of love and attention from the adults in their lives, it is not hard to imagine these children in bed together, finding mutual masturbation comforting and fun.

## ■ Prevention

Studies in the 1980s began to focus on sexual abuse of children and it became apparent quickly that among the young, especially those 7 years old or less, perpetrators were relatives or other people known to the child. Research has found that 99% of the perpetrators were known to the victim and 62% were either biological fathers or father-surrogates. Most incidents occurred in the child's home. Gradually, as children get older, go to school, participate in more activities away from home, and are supervised less closely, chances increase that they will encounter someone outside their homes who sexually abuses them (Finkelhor, 1986; Finkelhor, Hotaling, Lewis, & Smith, 1990; Reinhart, 1987).

Awareness of child sexual abuse in the general population increased in the mid-1980s. People were shocked and wanted to do something about it. Because parents had neither experience nor instruction in talking to their children about sexual matters, it is not surprising that, rather than methods that might encourage parents to discuss the facts of the problem with teachers, therapists, other adults, and finally with children, programs became popular that were supposedly designed to teach children to protect *themselves*. These programs succeeded in frightening young children about strangers, a meaningless word for a child under the age of 7. Strangers are uncommon perpetrators against all children, especially very young ones. Stranger perpetrators plan well, have the element of total surprise on their side, and no child or adult can defend against them. Children have been taught to "just say no" if someone touches areas "where you wear a bathing suit." This ignores the fact that children up to about 5 or 6 years old need help wiping themselves after a bowel movement. Children are instructed to tell their mothers about touches that "feel bad." But in many households, mothers are the people who tell young children what to do and not to do, applying punishment when needed (Graziano & Namaste, 1990).

Messages about sexual abuse are often delivered with a threatening and frightening demeanor, leaving many youngsters not at all sure who did wrong. Telling their mothers might invite punishment for not having obeyed. Children are also instructed to tell *someone*, if not their mothers, but often there is no one else who gives young children a chance to talk in private. Specifically, doctors, nurses, and teachers are always talking to parents and rarely inviting confidences from children. They appear to be the allies of parents. Children perceive correctly the existing identification between adults that excludes children. Added to this problem is that teachers are rarely taught to discuss with young children questions from the school program, nor what to say if children tell them about a sexual encounter. They may, in fact, become hysterical, especially if they had sexually abusive childhoods with which they have never come to terms. Obviously, this will frighten children, who will interpret tearful or hysterical reactions as "I must've done something wrong." However, advocates of such programs are nonetheless pleased with themselves, having convinced parents, teachers, and police that something useful was accomplished because now the children "know" and can "protect themselves."

Although the fact that sexual abuse is usually perpetrated by relatives and close family friends is widely understood and reported, it apparently has been ignored by most of the "prevention" programs. The emphasis was on family values during the 1980s and schools were not permitted to mention sexual abuse in the home. Of course, one wonders if parents were ever given any facts with which to make a decision regarding school discussion. Did they know that sexual abuse of young children is overwhelmingly a problem at home? Recently, a few prevention programs have made strides in teaching children about parent and relative mistreatment.

Talking about "good touch" and "bad touch," also common in prevention programs, is confusing language if the child is slapped, spanked, beaten, or sexually abused at home. It is difficult to tell children who have never known anything else that their parents are abusing them (Stein & Lewis, 1992). Most children, whether sexually or physically abused, remain intensely loyal to their parents and will deny mistreatment. These are the only parents they have ever known and the children are attached to them (even though the parenting is of poor quality). Abusers generally convince children of their own guilt, and prevention programs have made that worse. Children now have additional sources of guilt because they did not tell someone, nor did they shout "no," nor did they defend or protect themselves.

Household mistreatment of children clearly gets in the way of providing them with an avenue for seeking help. For many of their early years (and perhaps all through their lives), abused children have no awareness that they deserve to be treated better. Their self-esteem is damaged, and the more damaged it is, the more vulnerable they become to victimization by others. Also, prevention programs do not discuss with young children that other children may want to play games with them that are not good, perhaps dangerous, including sexual games among classmates, baby-sitters, siblings, and neighbors.

Incarcerated adult perpetrators of sexual crimes have taught us, through their therapists, important information about prevention that should be taught to parents. They look for likely victims, those who lack self-assurance and who seem to be lonely, available, or anxious. The typical process of grooming by these prospective perpetrators is thus: to become well acquainted, good friends, and trusted by the parents. They have a friendship interval, sometimes prolonged, before anything sexual is even suggested or tried (Berliner & Conte, 1990).

There are other kinds of attackers who are unseen strangers. They are rare, violent, and may abduct and kill. Adult males (such as Jeffrey Dahmer's victims) cannot defend against them and certainly little

*Among adults convicted of sex crimes, about 30% began offending before they were 9 years old.*

children cannot (Finkelhor, Hotaling, & Sedlak, 1992; Groth & Burgess, 1979). What is most shocking is hearing these convicts tell of their start as perpetrators. Among adults convicted of sex crimes, about 30%, certainly a significant number, began offending before they were 9 years old (Groth & Burgess, 1979; McGrath, 1990). Some adolescents recalled that they offended even at 3 and 4 years old (Johnson, 1991a).

Sexualized behavior is common in children who have been sexually abused (Corwin & Olafson, 1993). Before youngsters become sufficiently acculturated to realize that that behavior is inappropriate in public (usually before ages 5 to 7), they are often very open about replaying what was done to them (Gale et al., 1988). It is therefore a window of opportunity when children are not as well defended as they are in later years. Starting at age 5, or perhaps even earlier, a few will split the sexual experiences away from conscious memory because they are too painful. Later, many children are better at hiding their sexual preoccupation and their perpetration may not be noticed. They will not talk about their victimization; they may find it too embarrassing, or they believe the threats made against them. Conflicting feelings of guilt, shame, and confusion; of not really knowing whose fault it was; and past experiences in trying to tell someone often convince children that they will not be believed or that they will be punished. Children are accustomed to being blamed and criticized simply for being children: "How many times do I have to tell you?" "Can't you do anything right?" "What is the matter with you?" "Go to your room!" and so on. Thus children have powerful reasons for not saying anything about sexual abuse: They think the sexual abuse is probably their fault, too.

Young children speak in the language of action, not words, and teachers and other observers must learn to understand that form of communication, which does not stop in childhood. Sexually abused girls often become pregnant, not necessarily by the perpetrator but because they have become sexually active or promiscuous at an early age. Among teen prostitutes, both male and female, early sexual abuse is almost universal. In adulthood, there are those who remain sexually addicted and tell of their compulsion for sexual experiences. For some, the addiction is to child victims. Others react to their violation with symptoms that include depression, sometimes culminating in suicide; drug and alcohol problems; lack of social skills; and eating disorders. The treatment outcomes for sexual abuse victims and perpetrators leave much to be desired (Sanders, 1991; Simon, Salas, Kazniak, & Kahn, 1992).

In devising prevention strategies programs, adults who were child sexual abuse victims need to be included. Parents need help in dealing with sexual issues with their own children. Prevention also needs to proceed in medical settings with all parents because although sexual abuse is widespread, most adults have never discussed it with anyone and their own victimization will interfere with parenting (Cole, Woolger, Power, & Smith, 1992; Dempster & Roberts, 1991).

## ■ Very Young Perpetrators of Sexual Abuse

There is an increasing concern that very young children are behaving sexually, some very aggressively, toward other children who are usually smaller and younger still. For example, in view of such observations, Colorado amended its Child Protection Law in 1991 to mandate reporting of children under 10 years old who are sexually aggressive toward other children (Colorado House Bill 91-1002; 19-3-308 [5.3] [a] [child protection]). There are several reasons for this.

First, the law recognizes that sexually imitative or aggressive behavior is a common signal of a child's own sexual abuse. The younger the child, the stronger the connection between such behavior and the child's own victimization.

As a child becomes older, other reasons for wanting sexual domination of another child come into play, none of which bodes well for the child's future. Intervention is necessary for all such children. The need to report children can be readily translated into child protection: "Young sex offenders should always be viewed as past or current victims of sexual abuse" (Federal Bureau of Investigation, 1987, p. 10).

The victim children also need to be interviewed and counseled to avoid chronically worrying about or viewing themselves as victims, to gain the self-confidence to resist sexual advances and bullying from other children, to be able to seek help in the future, to discuss the event that occurred, to gain confidence, and even to try out ideas about how such victimization might be avoided in the future. How to avoid becoming a perpetrator needs to be addressed routinely in therapy.

Second, most states allow criminal prosecution after a child has turned 10 years of age. This age varies slightly between states. But letting a child act out sexually toward others while ignoring it for, say, 8 years, and then conferring criminal status on that child when a specific birthday passes, does not make sense. A better solution is to determine what can be done to alter the aggressive behavior as soon as it is observed or is reported for treatment.

Although more than 50% of adult sexual offenders begin their deviant behavior before they are 18 years old (Abel et al., 1987; Fromuth, Burkhart, & Jones, 1991; Simon et al., 1992), little is known statistically about child perpetrators becoming adult or adolescent offenders. There is evidence that sexual abuse of a male child heightens his risk of becoming an adult sex abuser (Vander Mey & Neff, 1982). Therapists who work with young, sexually aggressive children find that a significant number of them are addicted to the behavior. The youngsters report that thoughts of sexual acting out are constant and preoccupying, and when they are caught, scolded, or punished, excitement is heightened to plan and execute their next sexual assault. (This information is from verbal communication with teachers and social workers who are working in public schools and from therapists for sexually aggressive children.)

Third, it has been shown clearly that treatment of adult sexual offenders is not particularly successful. Many therapists involved in the treatment of perpetrators would agree that sex with children is an addiction for the perpetrator. Although people in sex addiction treatment programs feel they have success, the absence of recidivism cannot be accurately determined because children and perpetrators don't tell. Perpetrators silence their victims and hide their perpetration from adults who might be suspicious.

It is thought that about half of the adolescent offenders are treated successfully (Ryan, 1987). Follow-up is difficult because offense records are expunged when the offenders reach the age of 18. What becomes of their sexual deviancy and aggression remains only in self-reporting. To my knowledge, no long-term follow-up has been attempted in the past 5 to 6 years to ascertain if adolescents' treatment was sufficient to restrain them from reoffending in adulthood. It is, of course, very difficult to find out. Self-reporting reveals far more victimizations than were suspected, but its reliability is questionable (Abel et al., 1987; Fromuth et al., 1991; McGrath, 1990; Sanders, 1991).

One may argue that it is only fair to have the misdeeds of youth expunged, but it also keeps offenders from public scrutiny. When, in adulthood, they are caught in sexual exploitation of children, it would be helpful to know about their past histories of sexual paraphilias, especially because there are often many victims involved.

The hope for such a statute is that sexually aggressive children may be more amenable to treatment than adults or adolescents, and possibly stopped from adult perpetration. Issues of discovery and confidentiality will continue to plague the inquiry into how many children become adult perpetrators.

Much needs to be learned before we can stem this tide of sexual abuse of children by children who then grow up to be adult perpetrators. An understanding must be gained of the development of perpetrators of sexual abuse—the violence, coercion, and threats—by pursuing actively those young children who manifest such preoccupation. For example, while in therapy, one young boy who apparently clearly understood the message that his behavior was socially forbidden said he enjoyed it and saw no reason to stop. When he turned 10 years old, he commented that he was now old enough to be arrested and he thought he'd better rethink whether the fun outweighed the worry about having to go to jail!

The fourth and last consideration to be mentioned is the tremendous number of children victimized by adult perpetrators. The earlier the perpetrators are stopped, the fewer potential perpetrators will have been subsequently created (Finkelhor et al., 1990).

## ■ Sexual Titillation

During the Victorian era, anything sexual was neither mentioned nor sanctioned, at least officially. This was the prevalent attitude of the grandparents of the parents now raising children. The subject was regarded as unmentionable and unfortunately, two generations later, there has been little change. There has been much opposition to learning more about human sexuality, in part because the Victorian attitude became enshrined in church doctrine and gained religiously accepted status.

Today the grandchildren of the Victorians have little more knowledge, especially about dealing with the constant bombardment of information, images, and stories to which present-day children are exposed. We are in a time warp in which we have difficulty discussing sexual information even when it is ubiquitous in the lives of children.

We can tell children about the anatomy of sexual organs, but how do we explain that Daddy insists on having his *Playboy* magazines, or something really pornographic, in the house? How do we explain that Daddy can have these but that Junior is "bad" if he is found to be looking at this material while masturbating because he is considered a child? Scores of magazines not intended to stimulate or to cater to sexual topics nevertheless contain advertising that is provocative and sexually explicit. Sexual titillation is ever-present in television programming to which children might otherwise be appropriately exposed. Then there is also the auditory assault. One Sunday at 6:30 p.m. (certainly not too late for children), during a commercial break on *60 Minutes* (a "news magazine" that many families watch together), a female voice from an advertisement suddenly screamed hysterically at a child, "I can't tell you who your father was, I was raped." Especially in a mother-headed single parent household, the questions and answers needed might become quite complicated for a young child. Although anyone can turn off the television permanently, not everyone will. Children will visit other people's households.

Programs designed for children also have a lot of scary material in them. This is not really new. Among fairy tales, Grimm's are especially violent, scary, and often cruel, and they have been read to children for decades. Although the explicit sexual information is new, it is debatable if the information is worse than war, mayhem, or child murder, as in Snow White, Hansel and Gretel, Red Riding Hood, and others.

## ■ The Ramifications of Increased Sexual Information

Older professional literature emphasized the importance of listening for precocious knowledge and vocabulary about sex when interviewing alleged sex abuse victims: This was thought to enhance the credibility of the subject. More recently, however, investigators have had to struggle with a new problem. Adult cable television channels to which children have access often deal with very explicit sexual interaction and demonstrate behavior between sexual partners that children might imitate. Movie theaters are full of children, and even if the movie they came to see is suitable, often the advertisements that precede it are not. They may be extremely violent, and some mix violent and abusive sex with various other forms of violence. The advertisements are often of the most violent images of the entire previewed movie, and it is these scenes that are shown to unforewarned and unwilling viewers waiting for a family movie. As children are barraged with increasing amounts of violence and sex, it has become difficult to ascertain what is learned from personal experience and what is learned from exposure to observed behavior in real life.

My first exposure to a child learning from the media happened many years ago. A delightful 4-year-old girl was brought by her concerned mother to the Denver Crisis Center for a physical examination and an interview. Her mother noticed an increase in sexual knowledge after the child returned from a 3-week visit with her father. I watched this little girl perform what she had seen people do in a very pornographic movie. She commented: "And then they did this and then they did that" as she raised her legs, or her bottom, in the air, "and then he put it here and then he put it there," pointing to various parts of her anatomy. When contacted, the father admitted to viewing a pornographic videotape with the little girl, claiming he thought she would not understand and that therefore it would not harm her. The little girl was very clear throughout the interview that what she was telling us had not been done to her but that grown-up people in the television tape had done it.

What constitutes appropriate parental guidance? Differences of opinion are vast and range from not allowing anything sexual in the child's life, which probably cannot be done, to those who advocate, usually for their own pleasure, consensual sex starting at age 8 or 10 (as in the Man-Boy Love Organization).

In addition, it is far from settled how much sexuality is "normal." Visible expression of childhood sexuality is very much a part of the culture in which one lives. Not long ago, masturbation was considered punishable, although it is probably virtually universal. With it went punishment or harsh language about any kind of overt sexual behavior, resulting in cultural suppression.

Children learn what is thought to be acceptable behavior through a process of acculturation, or socialization. Initially, the adults who are the child's caretakers have the most influence on this process, but when a child goes to school, the peer group begins to assert an influence that grows with that child.

This probably led to Freud's use of the word "latency," the period of supposed abeyance of sexual curiosity in children. It is supposed to occur around ages 6 or 7 and 11 or 12. Probably, it actually described children who learned that sexual questions or behavior were deemed "bad" by the adults in their lives. What is purported "normal" sexual interest and "normal" sexual behavior in young children is determined by the responses of adults and where they happen to set boundaries. Young children are very aware of adults' body language, the visual and facial clues that tell them what is disapproved of, what is acceptable, and what is considered cute or funny. Continued study should improve the ability to respond appropriately, even at early childhood, because long before verbal language is really understood, children understand what is okay or not okay. At this time in our knowledge, masturbation is presumed to be "normal" and is observed in infancy. At about 3 years of age, children learn that it is not acceptable in public. Sexual feelings in the preschool years (ages 3 to 6) are common and are often expressed toward people they like, usually of the opposite sex. Adults sometimes complain that they find such attentions of young children uncomfortable because they are perceived as "seductive." A seductive quality in a child's behavior is much more pronounced in children who have been sexually abused.

Preschoolers and early-school-age children who are curious about each others' genitalia, and the "I'll show you mine if you'll show me yours" game, as well as some touching to see what a penis or scrotum feels like, are considered normal, although they probably were not 50 or more years ago.

School-age children often discuss and joke about sexual matters, which seems imitative of observed adults. It is a hallmark of acceptable sexual behavior that children involved in such behavior do so with a sense of fun and openness.

The term "girlfriend" (or "boyfriend") enters a child's vocabulary very early. It usually appears before 5 or 6 years old and is introduced by someone such as an older sibling, a parent, or a friend in commenting about two little children of the opposite sex who like to play together.

Without such comment from their elders, the appellation would not emerge, but clearly there are feelings of attraction in preschool-age children.

Adults report "French kissing" to Child Protective Services (CPS) because they find it unacceptable in childhood and regard it as indicative of a possibly inappropriate sexual experience. However, that will probably change if the age at which it is acceptable is lowered. On television, all kissing clearly is with open mouths, which children see and assume is the norm. They try it out before or by the age of "dating," which is quite common now at 11 and 12 years of age. Early dating is encouraged by many parents who think it's cute, who were not "popular" and want to make sure their children enjoy popularity, or for other reasons. Other parents may think it inappropriate and complain about having to go along with a perceived norm because "everybody" does it. Children have a way of making parents feel guilty about "being the only ones who won't let me _____."

Children reach biological maturity earlier than they did 2 generations ago, which is at odds with their needing to remain in an educational setting until they are at least 18 years old. Things have changed: In 1900, the average educational attainment in the United States was third grade! This poses a very specific problem that should, but does not seem to, influence societal and cultural objectives for messages about sex to preschool- and early-school-age children, as well as to older children. In schools and other places where children are together with observant adults, it is not uncommon to hear reports that children around 9 years old are experimenting sexually among same-age peers.

Sexual experimentation leads to babies unless educators teach the connection between intercourse, babies, and birth control. Sexually transmitted diseases are finally getting some attention because of AIDS, but still there is very little knowledge transmitted about other diseases, particularly chlamydia and gonorrhea, which can cause infertility, or papilloma virus, which is extremely painful to treat and, if not treated, may be a precursor to cervical cancer.

The alternative is what has been observed for the past 25 years: babies born to very young mothers and doomed to poverty, and many young women with fertility problems from venereal diseases. An appropriate and meaningful educational effort should begin in early life and not at a later point, when the children at risk are already sexually active.

## ■ Identifying Sexually Aggressive Children

There are behaviors that most observers will agree are not and should not be considered normal among children. A brief description of such behaviors is anything done to another child that is aggressive and unwanted by the recipient, who could then be labeled a victim of a perpetrator.

Many schools accept that every week or two "it's flippin' Friday," when the boys flip up the girls' skirts and the girls learn that they must wear pants to school on that day. The schools know, the parents know, the children know, but no one takes action until someone, usually a parent, decides it's not right and puts a temporary end to it. Clearly, it is an aggressive act that among adults in the workplace would be labeled sexual harassment. The argument one hears about it is that the girls love it, it shows they are popular, it's just play, and so on, but in reality, it is yet another example that confuses many adults about what is appropriate for children. Perpetrators of all sexual aggression quickly claim that their victims were agreeable and did not object or resist, that, in fact, they had asked for it and enjoyed it.

Thus we find ourselves with young children in the age-old double bind as to the contribution the victim made to an instance of inappropriate sexual interaction. Seeing that older boys are not punished for flipping skirts, a child may begin to pull down underwear! What might come next? Perhaps pinching or "goosing" other children? Soon, when confronted, children will respond along the lines of, "She did it first," "He started it," "I'm only doing what everybody else does," and so forth. Adults who deal with children need to agree on clear, consistent, and more or less universal messages so that children know what is not permitted when they come to school or gather in other social situations. Adults need to send a clear and unambiguous signal that aggressive behavior, which includes sexual aggression, is not permitted.

In pondering the respective roles of aggressor and victim, perhaps we should study the power structure between the children before deciding which behavior is detrimental. For instance, one girl claimed that she was sexually abused in her foster home by their adopted son, who had been sexually abused in his biological family. Skepticism around her allegation concerned the fact that the boy was almost 2 years younger than the girl. This is a perfect example of unequal power because, notwithstanding her older age, the girl had only just arrived and was a frightened stranger with no power in the household. The boy had been there for several years and had been adopted. He threatened her and she complied because he was in a more powerful position. This can occur with same-age children if one is, for instance, the basketball star and the other would like to be chosen for the team.

For investigators of child-to-child sexual abuse, the issue of power, and therefore control, is very important to study and understand. The need for power and control is the motivation in most adult rapes, and children may have similar needs.

> *The need for power and control is the motivation in most adult rapes, and children may have similar needs.*

Some children who have been victims will try to reenact their sexual abuse by getting another child to act the part of the perpetrator. This may be how a "sexual epidemic" develops in a classroom, much the way an epidemic like measles spreads. One sexual abuse victim can involve others, who in turn involve others, and the entire class, school bus, or athletic team will be playing at sex with no readily apparent initial source of the behavior (Cantwell, 1988).

When inquiring about the activities of sexually interactive children, understand that a penis is not required for the initiation of such activities. One mother noticed that her child, a little girl who had been sexually used by her father for about 4 years, was bringing home money from school. A complaint came from school, so the child, mother, and teacher conferred. The young girl had been selling favors to the boys; they paid her different amounts depending on what she would do for them. The boys promptly went to other little girls to ask if they would do the same. It turned out that most of the second grade had become involved. Ages 3 to 7 may be the last feasible and convenient time to alter this aggression, even though one cannot know how many of the children will go on to become adolescent or adult perpetrators.

Most studies have indicated the predominance of female victims of sexual abuse, but the statistical difference between the sexes may not be as great as originally thought (Finkelhor, 1986; Friedrich, 1993; Gale et al., 1988). In fact, boys tell less often, or they tell later in life, thus eventually making statistics more evenly distributed. This has been revealed by surveys of adults who are asked about sexual encounters before age 18.

Although there are more female child victims, there continues to be a dearth of adult females reported as perpetrators of sexual abuse.

However, articles about convicted and incarcerated rapists indicate that of those who experienced childhood sexual abuse, about half were abused by females. A large percentage of those were from incestuous abuse (Groth & Burgess, 1979). The significance of this is that women have been recognized far more frequently as childhood victims of older males, and treatment has been concentrated on their victimization, ignoring their possible role as perpetrators. Particularly important is that perpetration is not infrequent among mothers, although often not recognized (Faller, 1984, 1988).

Young girls complain that their mothers insist on vaginal douches, take them to colonic irrigation parlors, examine their genitalia daily to make sure they were not molested at school, and insert fingers to make sure they were not damaged. These kinds of behaviors are less frequently reported by boys, although some certainly are in bed with their mothers at perhaps inappropriately late ages.

## ■ What Can Be Done?

The Colorado law that mandates the reporting of sexually aggressive children is receiving mixed reviews. When teachers in some counties report children, they find CPS agencies that are able and interested in responding, whereas this is not the case in other counties. All public agencies have suffered shortages of money and personnel. The overwhelming need is to attend to the criminal court cases. Sexual abuse by other children, after all, is only "kid stuff," or "sex play."

The public needs to be educated to sharpen awareness of the harm done by child perpetrators and their potential to produce more and more victims who also might become perpetrators. At present, little is done if the parent of a sexually aggressive child simply refuses to allow an interview, saying that the allegations are untrue, that some other child initiated the sexualized interaction, or that the other parent is always causing trouble.

Obviously, an uncooperative parent may have a very personal reason for not allowing an interview; most sexual abuse of young children occurs in the home. Unfortunately, it is extremely rare that a court order is obtained requiring a child to be interviewed or ordered into treatment. Better information might lead the public to demand early intervention.

Meanwhile, such children continue to create problems at school. A teacher is obviously frustrated when dealing with children who perform sexual acts in the classroom, sometimes on a daily basis. For example, in a classroom of 10 emotionally disturbed boys, ages 7 to 9, the school needed to add a full-time aide in order to avoid having sex as the only subject discussed in that classroom! A half-time social worker came in to begin therapy, but two of the boys told her that the sexual behavior was totally preoccupying, and she realized that these boys had a sexual addiction.

Schools exist to teach, but these children seriously disrupt that mission. Therefore, school seems the ideal place to institute intervention. In schools, an arrangement with a mental health clinic might be the best way to create group therapy for all children who aggressively act out (sexually or otherwise). Alternatively, schools may wish to train their social workers to conduct such groups. If therapy were available in school, it would eliminate the complaint of working parents that the cost or the time commitment in taking their children to therapy is prohibitive.

Headstart, a prekindergarten program for disadvantaged children, has social workers who could also receive such training. It would be a good place for therapy because at Headstart, children often get initial exposure to the kind of group they will encounter in school, and the program concerns itself specifically with all aspects of school readiness, including behavior toward other children and adults.

Initially, however, therapy may not be as effective as a clear and consistent "no" from the teacher. The schools need help in learning how to deal with disruptive children and those who hurt other children.

Fundamentally, aggressive children who inflict hurt are symptomatic. They represent and reflect a societal state of affairs of rampant violence that is continually portrayed and reinforced in the mass media. In the long run, these aggressive children, if incarcerated, will be hurt as much as they've hurt their victims. Schools must include standards that do not allow students to hurt others. To protect others, sexualized behavior that is intractable will need to be treated by experts as soon as possible, by court order if necessary.

Unresolved is what should be taught to children about sexuality. Is it harmful to expose them to sexual knowledge early in their school years? What should we say about what adults do? What is appropriate for teenagers? At what age is sexual intercourse okay? Today, children make these decisions with little input from knowledgeable, responsible sources. They are ruled by peer pressure and rely on peer-perpetuated myths to make the decision to become sexually active.

Some school systems have initiated programs to teach appropriate information; unfortunately, many have not. Involving parents in curriculum decisions is another strategy gaining popularity. In areas where fundamentalist religious groups are well organized, their opinions prevail, and although they are often in the minority, they prevent sex education not only for their own children, but for all the others as well.

The high rates of teen pregnancy and sexually transmitted diseases (STD) in the early 1970s were lowered through attention and the resulting preventive efforts. The 1980s, however—the decade of "just say no" and "abstinence is best"—saw a rise in these rates, which are an excellent barometer for the spread of AIDS.

## ■ Discussion and Possibilities for Treatment

Ryan et al. (1989) outlined an exact approach to training teachers and school social workers to respond to children whose actions fit the terms "sexually aggressive," "sexually acting out," "deviant," and "exploitative." Unless trained, teachers may ignore what they observe due to their own discomfort with childhood sexuality, or they may react too angrily, which confuses children. Teachers need to have their behavior labeled and discussed with them. Most young children will behave sexually at some time in their childhood, observed by neighbors or schools, which can be prohibited by saying, "Please, don't do that here." Just as playing ball indoors is forbidden because it might break a lamp, aggressive behavior is forbidden because it will hurt the victims of it. "You would not like it if someone did it to you."

Most young children exhibit developmentally normal sexualized behaviors. A 2-year-old who takes off his pants and brags about the use of his penis for urination is normal developmentally. If the same behavior occurs in kindergarten, it is no longer normal. We then wonder about the lack of expected socialization, indicative more of neglect than sexual abuse. When the original reprimand, repeated, does not stop the child's objectionable behavior, we need to spend some time finding out why the behavior is so attractive. Children taking their own and others' clothes off and touching their genitalia, at an age when curiosity about their bodies should be satisfied, exemplifies behavior that moves from "developmentally expected" to "worrisome" as it becomes repetitive. Sexualized games that exclude other kinds of play, especially if they are also secretive because they are understood as forbidden, introduce an addictive component already discussed as common in adult perpetrators. Adding coercion or force to the scenario, thus frightening another child into complying with demands to play at imitative or intrusive sexual intercourse, means that the situation has moved to the most serious level and is clearly abnormal. Intervention is needed to prevent further escalation.

Recently, Children's World (1993) sponsored a conference in Denver in which attendees attempted to label and define sexualized behaviors of children. Several terms were agreed on. The first was "developmentally appropriate." The second, "worrisome" or "allows for a wait-and-see attitude," is the most inclusive because, realistically, there are many that cannot be categorized with our present knowledge. If requested to stop, most children will, but some will escalate to more serious offending behavior. These children move into the third category, where everyone would agree that intervention is needed. These behaviors are serious and require action. A consensus document including definitions and recommended actions will become available as a result of the conference.

Some private schools, such as day care or nursery schools, have the option of excluding children who are disruptive, aggressive, and hurtful to others. Not so the public schools. Even when these children are placed in special classrooms for emotionally disturbed children, sexual aggression continues and involves or affects all of the children. In addition, CPS could not handle the number of cases it would need to if all sexualized children were reported.

Public schools are justifiably reluctant to address the problem because their assigned task is to teach, not to provide mental health treatment. Treatment of children is usually not needed initially, but classroom teachers at all early childhood and elementary levels can learn new techniques of labeling and responding to inappropriate sexual behavior; in other words, primary prevention.

Lévi-Strauss states that

> local specification of incest is one of the defining characteristics of human culture. Central to the identity of each culture is the unique set of proscriptions that it endorses, as well as the specific methods that it employs to transmit and enforce those choices from one generation to another. (quoted in Mulhern, 1990, p. 265)

Mulhern reports that the Chulupi Indians of Paraguay transmit information and approved social attitudes regarding incest through a story. The Chulupi perceive intergenerational sexual desire as a fact of human nature, but they also prohibit acting on it. Their tale provokes riotous laughter from all members of the tribe, and its telling can be requested by anyone at any time. Although its educational purpose is not overt, it is, nevertheless, very effective. It is the tale of a ridiculous, bumbling, shaman grandfather, who is such a fool and a failure as a credible member of society that he actually acts on his desire to have sex with his granddaughter. This teaching myth conveys the blamelessness of the victim, the granddaughter, who is raped by her grandfather. The grandfather tells how he needs her to do this and that because he is so old and helpless, and he ultimately puts her in a helpless position, after which he rapes her. Thus the story clearly warns of a likely perpetrator methodology; it also upholds that doing the forbidden has risks. The painful injuries inflicted on the grandfather by a second granddaughter, who escapes him, and those inflicted by his wife, who has been told of his actions, also convey that the victim does not get into trouble as a result of talking (Mulhern, 1990).

By contrast, our sexually secretive culture produces adults with a poor knowledge of sexuality in childhood, adolescence, and adulthood. Not talking about sex has not made it socially more manageable—probably less so (Simkins, 1991).

Perhaps, in our own way, we could also develop stories to tell children about sex, about what is appropriate and what is forbidden. As it is, normal sexual desire, thoughts, and ambivalence are not discussed. My suggestion is that we at least begin to discuss among ourselves the things that have happened to many of us: being confronted by men who exposed their genitalia to us when we were little; being embarrassed by crude, suggestive remarks; having uncles who looked at us with a peculiar, leering smile or gym teachers who "accidentally" grabbed the wrong body part; encountering unauthorized visitors in our bathrooms; getting tickled by a bigger child, which hurt and was sexually suggestive; and so forth.

Ambivalence is a human emotion rarely mentioned between adults and children. It should be discussed extensively because it causes unnecessary guilt feelings when children and adults suffer from "evil" thoughts. Our teaching needs to emphasize that "thinking" is separate from "action." Also, children can be taught to understand that thinking and imagining are private, but that some things must not be acted on because of societal prohibition.

Finkelhor and Lewis's telephone survey in 1988, averaging across two samples, showed that 10% of adult men admitted to having sexually abused a child. Fromuth et al. (1991) found that among the college men who responded to a questionnaire, the incidence was about 3% and that all were 16 to 17 years old when they molested. She questions if there were more "hidden" molesters. One wonders if these molesters, who are capable of admitting to it and who, from other test results, are people not much different from nonmolesters, might also have been prevented from molesting if there were more teaching and openness. Ninety percent reported mildly abusive behavior and possibly regarded it as fun for the younger child as well. What if they had been instructed at some point about the lasting harm that would be done to the younger, less powerful child in such situations? Half of the victims reported one incident. Half were victimized as children, and always by relatives. No questions were asked about whether they perpetrated before age 16 (Fromuth et al., 1991).

Sexual abuse victims get caught up in criminal cases if the abusers are older by at least 3 to 5 years and if there is enough evidence to convict the perpetrators, which means that the children must be old enough, smart enough, and reliable enough to be believed. The children who are sexually misused often do not fulfill these qualifications or do not tell, and they are never told anything about the typical behavior of perpetrators. Therefore, they fall prey to repeated victimization. As stated earlier, teaching self-defense is contraindicated. Societal prohibitions, which we are expected to obey, need to be taught with precision and clarity to all children and should include those prohibitions concerning sexual behavior. Sexual capacity is as inborn and natural as its expression is learned and cultural. Schools acculturate children in perhaps every other area, from teaching them to pledge allegiance to the flag to teaching them not to lie or steal. We need to acculturate children sexually as well. Those who were sexually abused may recognize a wrong committed against them, and they may begin to talk about it instead of acting it out and passing it on to others. Those who cannot stop acting on the modeled behavior need more treatment.

Treatment for sexual abuse includes learning about and feeling sympathy for victims, which must be translated into the actual events of asking forgiveness of victims and making restitution (Ryan, 1987; Smets & Cebula, 1987). Absence of empathy is probably the common root of child maltreatment (Jones & Alexander, 1987; Steele, 1987), and this aspect of adolescent treatment protocols will hopefully prevent them from becoming adult abusers. Those unable to apologize to victims are found to have a higher incidence of recidivism.

Empathy develops in the context of healthy bonding, in which an infant grows to trust its primary caretaker(s) to provide and protect. In short, the next generation benefits in many ways when treatment is instituted early in the lives of young perpetrators. It not only protects future victims, it helps perpetrators develop the empathic feelings needed for good parenting. In neglectful or abusive households, bonding and attachment develop in unhealthy pathological patterns, such as role reversal, or in cases where children must cater to parents' needs or else face severe punishment.

More teaching is needed to help professionals in contact with babies and toddlers recognize healthy, as opposed to pathological, tendencies of parent-child relationships. We have come full circle: To have good parenting, one needs to have experienced it; otherwise, the unhealthy relationships in which children are reared are brought into the next generation as the norm.

Preventing, helping, correcting, reparenting, and reeducating have all been tried with mixed success. If we work at intervention, we might get better at it earlier in children's lives, improving the quality of parenting. Perhaps it will prevent the victimization of others.

# 5

# When the Offender Is a Child

## *Identifying and Responding to Juvenile Sexual Abuse Offenders*

### Jacqueline Jackson Kikuchi

Although there may be some disagreement about both the actual and disclosed rates of occurrence of child sexual abuse (for a review, see Urquiza & Keating, 1990), most people agree that it is common. A wealth of information on the prevention, intervention, and treatment of child sexual abuse for children, parents, and professionals is commonly available and widely disseminated. It seems that most people now strongly believe that it is inappropriate for adults to involve themselves sexually with children and that adults who are sexually involved with children should be held accountable for their actions.

However, in working with tens of thousands of children, teens, parents, teachers, and professionals in the past few years, I have become aware that we, as a society, are tolerant of sexual abuse between children or adolescents, even when there is a considerable age difference between the children or adolescents or when some of those involved clearly did not consent to the activity. In fact, we are often more tolerant of sexually abusive behaviors of children and adolescents than we are of their normal sexual behaviors. We have all heard others respond to abusive sexual activity by young children with "They were just playing doctor," "He/she was just curious," or "Boys will be boys." If the behavior is recognized as abusive, it is usually ignored with the rationalization that "there is nothing I can do about it." Unwanted grabbing, pinching, peeping, teasing, pulling down pants or pulling up skirts, and harassment are all common activities among young people from preschool to college. In general, sexual offenses by children and adolescents are minimized, rationalized, ignored, and denied by society.

I am sure that part of the acceptance comes from the knowledge that some sexual activity between children is normal and that it is not always easy to discern the difference between normal and abnormal sexual activity involving children or adolescents. I am also sure that some of the acceptance comes from the fact that we do not want to believe that adolescents and children can be sexual abuse offenders. Although many cases of sexual activity between children and adolescents are normal, there is also much sexual behavior that goes beyond what is considered normal and requires assessment, intervention, and possibly treatment for the young people involved.

Sexual abuse offenses committed by children and adolescents have lasting consequences for both the victims and the offenders. Studies have found that children who are sexually abused by other children suffer the same types and severity of negative consequences as children who are sexually abused by adults (Haugaard & Tilly, 1988; Lorado, 1982). Most adult sexual offenders admit that they began sexually offending as children and adolescents (Abel et al., 1987; Longo & Groth, 1983). Longo and McFadin (1981) and Longo and Groth (1983) found that juvenile offenders committing sexual assaults and rapes usually began with hands-off offenses such as exposing, peeping, and harassment.

The reinforcing nature of sexual behaviors may lead to a child's or adolescent's deviant sexual acts becoming repetitive and ingrained. These abusive patterns can become habitual and may progress to incorporate more deviant sexual acts (Ryan, Lane, Davis, & Isaac, 1987). The positive feelings of power and control felt by the young offender combine with the physical gratification of the sexual activity to make the perceived advantages of the abuse outweigh the potential negative consequences (Ryan et al., 1987). Young offenders need to be identified and treated early: By adolescence, many offending children have abused more than one child and the deviant sexual behaviors are often well established (Henderson, English, & MacKenzie, 1988).

The responses to childhood sexual activity, whether normal or abusive, by both other children and adults, have a great impact on children's values and their attitudes toward sexuality. Responses to normal sexual activities that indicate to children that they have done something bad or dirty may lead to feelings that they and their bodies are bad. It may also lead to the feeling that they cannot talk about sexuality, neither normal nor abusive. When the activity is sexually abusive and the behavior is ignored, both victims and offenders receive the impression that the activity is acceptable (Kikuchi, 1988).

Clearly, we need to improve our skills at identifying and responding to both normal and abusive sexual activity in children. We also need to improve our skills at identifying and responding to those children who are at risk of continuing to sexually abuse others so that they can be given appropriate treatment.

In this chapter, I discuss the differences between normal and abnormal sexual activity in children and adolescents and the incidence of sexual abuse by child and adolescent offenders. I also recommend education strategies that I have found to be effective for both children and adults regarding sexual abuse awareness, prevention, and intervention.

## ■ Normal Versus Abusive Sexual Activity

Some sexual activity between children is considered normal. How should one decide if a specific sexual activity between children is normal or abusive? Several models have been developed to help us discern the difference between normal and abnormal sexual activity in children and adolescents.

Some professionals have suggested that the difference in the ages of the children involved in the sexual activity can be used to assess if the behavior is abusive. It has typically been accepted that in sexual activity between children who are 5 or more years apart in age, the older child is abusing the younger even if the activity is considered normal for similarly aged children (Watkins & Bentovim, 1992). However, other studies have suggested that an age difference of 2 or more years could indicate an abusive situation (Johnson, 1988; Watkins & Bentovim, 1992).

The type of sexual activity also may be used to determine if the situation is normal or sexually abusive. A normal activity is curiosity about another child's genitalia with mutual undressing. However, oral-genital contact and penetration of the vaginal or anal opening with fingers or objects is abnormal in preadolescent children (Cantwell, 1988).

Crisci and Brown (personal communication, 1992) examined the motivation, the relationships, the activities, and the affects of the children involved in sexual behavior to determine if the activity is part of normal sexual development or is sexually abusive (see Table 5.1). Normal sexual activity in children is motivated by curiosity, provides mutual interest and has mutual consent, and is "fun" or "silly" for the children involved. However, if coercion, bullying, or a lack of parity is involved; if the activity is an reenactment of adult sexual activity; or if one or more of the children feels fear, shame, or discomfort, then the situation probably should be considered abusive.

Clearly, juvenile sexual offending cannot be defined by just the behaviors involved. The nature of the relationship between the victim and offender, the dynamics of the actions, and the impact on the victim must also be considered. Haugaard and Tilly (1988) found that in many cases, the victims' reactions could not be predicted by the type of sexual activity in which they had engaged; they found that the atmosphere surrounding the sexual activity had the greatest influence on the victims' feelings and responses to the situation.

Ryan (1991a) defines a juvenile sex offender as a minor who commits any sexual act against the victim's will, without consent, or with any type of aggression or threats of aggression, regardless of the age of the victim. Lorado (1982) suggests that if deception, intimidation, or force was used, the act should be considered sexually abusive.

I suggest that the situation be examined in three steps, which I will present and then discuss. First, determine if there was any type of force or power used in the activity or generally in the relationship. Second, if no apparent force or power was used, assess if all of the young people involved consented to the activity. Third, evaluate if the activity may be considered normal sexual activity for the age of the children involved.

The activity should be considered sexual abuse if power is a part of the sexual activity or relationship. Power may include physical strength, force, threats, or weapons. More subtle but more commonly used types of force in sexual abuse include a misuse of trust, tricks, threats, blackmail, peer pressure, differences in knowledge due to age or mental

**TABLE 5.1** Guidelines for Assessing the Nature of Sexual Behavior
              in Children

| Areas | Normal | Abusive |
|-------|--------|---------|
| Motivation | Curiosity | Coercion-based |
| Relationship | Mutual interest and consent | Bullying and lack of parity |
| Activity | Looking, touching | Explicit reenactment of adult sexual activity |
| Effect | Often fun, silly | Fear, shame, discomfort |
| Example | "I'll show you mine, if you'll show me yours" | "Having sex" |

SOURCE: Copyright 1984 by Geraldine Crisci. Revised, 1991, 1992 by Crisci & Brown. Reprinted by permission

abilities, and bribes (including friendship). Abusive sexual behavior is not limited to behavior with physical contact between the parties. Language, peeping, exposing, and posting of pornography can also be abusive.

> *Abusive sexual behavior is not limited to behavior with physical contact between the parties.*

It should be remembered throughout the assessment that victims sometimes say "yes" or go along with an activity without resistance as a response to the force or power used. Therefore, a response of "yes," an absence of "no," or a lack of resistance to force or power does not imply that that young person truly consented to the situation.

Even if no apparent force or power was used, we must consider the context. When assessing consent in juvenile sexual activity, a practical, but remarkably robust guideline to use is whether we feel that the children could have said "no" and everything would still have been well. Children often will comply with another's demands out of fear or because they did not feel they had another option. It is important to remember that compliance and cooperation are different from consent. Consent requires that all parties must have knowledge, understanding, and choice in the activities. We typically instruct young people to ignore behavior that makes them feel uncomfortable. Therefore, ignoring a behavior should be considered the same as responding negatively to the behavior. Although young people often do not respond negatively to sexual harassment and teasing, the activity is rarely consented to. When asked, most victims will respond that they would not have chosen to be involved in the harassment or teasing.

If no force or power was used and all parties consented, examine the activity to determine if it is considered normal or abnormal sexuality for children of a given age. Making such a decision is difficult because discussions of normal sexual behavior for children are controversial and conflict-ridden (see the chapter by Cantwell in this volume). Many adults resist accepting that any sexual behaviors in children are normal. Published research and information on normal sexual activity in children and adolescents are scarce.

A review of published observations and research on normal sexual development in infancy and early childhood is provided by Martinson (1991). He concludes that although there is no agreement on what is considered age-appropriate sexual behavior in children, for young children, the primary goal of normal sexual behavior is usually exploration rather than sexual gratification.

Sgroi, Bunk, and Wabrek (1988) discuss a variety of behaviors that should be considered normal for children of various ages. Children from birth to age 5 are primarily interested in touching the sexual parts of their bodies and looking at and touching the private parts of others' bodies if given the opportunity. Children ages 6 to 10 masturbate but with more secrecy than younger children. Elementary school-age children are also likely to create opportunities to view the private parts of adults or children or to create games with peers that require undressing and possibly touching the private parts. Preadolescents and adolescents continue to masturbate; to have an intense interest in viewing others' bodies, especially members of the opposite sex; and to develop close relationships with others that may include a range of touching experiences. Sgroi et al. (1988) emphasize that it is *not* normal for preadolescents or adolescents to be involved in any type of sexual behavior with preschool- or elementary school-age children.

Miller, Christopherson, and King (1993) describe normal and abnormal sexuality in adolescents. They point out that as children become adolescents, the range and frequency of normal sexual behaviors increase. The development of new normal sexual behaviors in adolescents progresses from hand-holding to sexual intercourse. It is again emphasized that nonconsensual, coercive, aggressive, or exploitative sexual behaviors should be considered sexual abuse.

# ■ Incidence of Child Offending

Several studies have suggested that child sexual abuse committed by children is quite common. A study by Deisher, Wenet, Paperney, Clark, and Fehrenbach (1982) found that 20% percent of all rapes and 30% to 50% of child sexual assaults were committed by adolescent offenders. Drawing on data of disclosures of sexual abuse, Ryan (1991b) estimates that at least 8% of all males and at least 5% to 7% of all females will be sexually abused by a child or adolescent before the age of 18.

Between 1988 and 1991, the Rhode Island Rape Crisis Center presented its Adolescent Assault Awareness program to approximately 18,000 adolescents in grades 4 to 12. After the workshops, 1,720 adolescents came to a private question time to disclose that they had experienced at least one incidence of child sexual assault as defined by Rhode Island laws (physical touching or penetration of the sexual parts of the body without consent; there may or may not be force involved). It was never suggested or implied to the students that during the question time they should disclose that they had been sexually assaulted; they were told only that we were available if they had anything they wanted to talk about privately. Of the adolescents who participated in the workshops, 13.3% of the females and 5.8% of the males disclosed that they had experienced at least one sexual assault as defined by Rhode Island laws. Sixty-eight percent of the disclosed assaults were committed by an offender under the age of 18, and 8% of the assaults by an offender under the age of 13. Nine percent of the girls and 4% of the boys who participated in the workshops disclosed being sexually assaulted by someone under the age of 18. A comparison of age groups of victims versus age groups of offenders for the four victim-offender gender categories is presented in Figures 5.1 through 5.4.

The most common assault disclosed was a female assaulted by a male offender (Figure 5.1); 1,169 girls disclosing being assaulted by male offenders. The offender was under the age of 13 in 8% of the assaults, between ages 13 and 15 in 32% of the assaults, ages 16 or 17 in 25% of the assaults, between ages 18 and 22 in 18% of the assaults, and over age 22 in 10% of the assaults. Thirteen- to 15-year-olds were the most common offenders reported by girls assaulted between the ages of 3 and 15. Male offenders ages 16 or 17 were most commonly reported by girls assaulted at ages 16 or 17. In general, girls reported being abused most commonly by males near their own age.

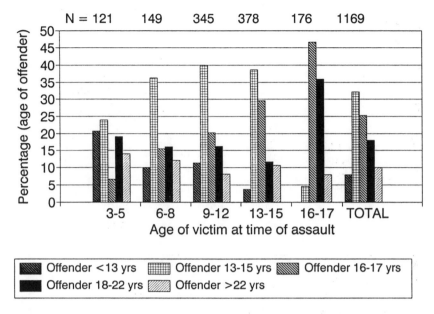

**Figure 5.1.** Sexual Assaults on Female Victims by Male Offenders

Male victims also reported that their offenders were usually male. Four hundred forty-eight boys disclosed being assaulted by male offenders (Figure 5.2). The offender was under age 13 in 6% of the assaults, ages 13 to 15 in 39% of the assaults, ages 16 or 17 in 23% of the assaults, ages 18 to 22 in 18% of the assaults, and over age 22 in 9% of the reported assaults. In the disclosures of male victims, the offender was most commonly a boy age 13 to 15 when the victim was age 3 to 12. The most common offender of 13- to 15-year-old boys was age 16 or 17, and the disclosed offenders were equally distributed between the three older age groups when the victim was age 16 to 18. Typically, males disclosed being assaulted by males who were slightly older than themselves.

In 6% of the disclosed assaults, the offender was female. Thirty-three girls (Figure 5.3) and 70 boys (Figure 5.4) disclosed being sexually assaulted by female offenders. In general, the ages of the offenders are fairly evenly distributed across all the age groups regardless of the age of the victim. However, no cases were reported in which a female assaulted a victim older than herself.

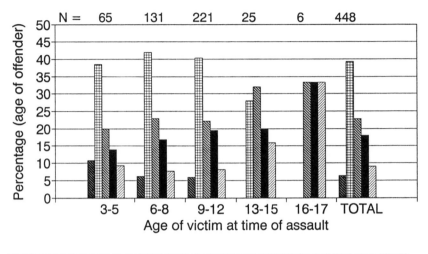

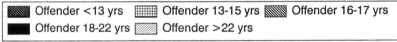

**Figure 5.2.** Sexual Assaults on Male Victims by Male Offenders

To summarize the findings: Young children are sexually assaulting other children; some of these assaults are rapes; and both males and females are offending as well as being assaulted.

## ■ Learning to Identify and Respond to Juvenile Offending

Judging by the number of juvenile offenders reported, we need to improve society's awareness of and responses to juvenile sexual abuse offending. Child sexual abuse prevention and awareness programs need to educate children, adolescents, and adults on the issues and incidence of sexual abuse offending by juveniles. Adults need to be informed as to how to identify and respond to normal and abnormal sexual behavior in children and adolescents, and young people need to learn how to respond to peers who are sexually abusive.

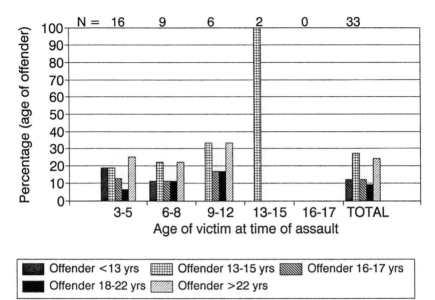

Figure 5.3. Sexual Assaults on Female Victims by Female Offenders

### Education for Children and Adolescents

Most popular education programs on sexual abuse awareness and prevention for children and adolescents present scenarios in which the offenders are adults or at least much older than the victims. If the disclosures in Rhode Island are representative of child sexual assault situations (and there is no reason to believe that they are not), awareness and prevention programs should focus on both adult and juvenile offenders. Young people need to know that a situation can be sexual abuse even if the offender is the same age as the victim.

Young people should be taught to deal with the peer pressure, threats, and bribes that are often a part of sexually abusive behaviors in adolescents. "Everyone else is doing it," "We won't be your friend if you don't do it," or "If you want to be part of the group you need to do it," are typical types of force used when juveniles abuse peers. Children and adolescents need to be able to recognize their peers' tactics as forceful and to realize that it is both acceptable and healthy to resist. Seeing adults modeling such behavior, in both real-life and role-play

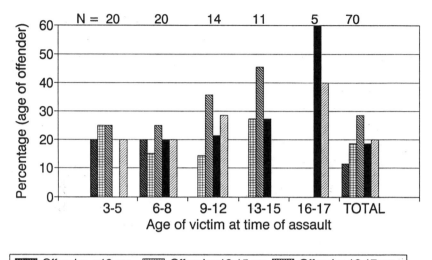

**Figure 5.4.** Sexual Assaults on Male Victims by Female Offenders

situations, helps children and adolescents to be assertive against force-ful behaviors from peers. Children and adolescents also need to learn that teasing and harassment, although common, are not acceptable or healthy sexual activities.

> *Children and adolescents need to be able to recognize their peers' tactics as forceful and to realize that it is both acceptable and healthy to resist.*

Children and adolescents also need to learn about normal sexuality. If they do not receive information about what is normal, then they cannot distinguish what is abnormal. Sexual abuse by juveniles is often minimized or dismissed by peers because they assume that the behavior is normal. The media often present sexually abusive behaviors by adolescents and young adults as normal. Young people who are left to learn about sexuality from the media naturally make the assumption that they and others should be behaving in the ways depicted. Information about normal sexuality should be followed by discussion about the media's portrayal of sexuality, with an emphasis on distinguishing between normal and abusive sexual behaviors. The elements of force, power, and consent should be the focus of these discussions.

Children and adolescents need to learn how to respond to peer sexual offending, not only when they are the victims of such behaviors, but also when they observe such activity in their peers. Even when young people are able to recognize sexual offending by peers, they are likely to ignore the behavior. When the behaviors are ignored, the victims and the offenders assume that their peers are supporting the abusive behavior.

Recent programs, such as the Rhode Island Rape Crisis Center's "No More Abuse" program for children and adolescents and the Committee For Children's "No More Victims, No More Victimizers," stress to the participants that they need to respond to inappropriate behavior from their peers even if adults appear to ignore or minimize the behavior. The "No More Abuse" program works with children to help them develop methods for interacting with abusive peers. The students are guided by the facilitators in developing a variety of responses to deal with the whole continuum of abusive behaviors. Poster contests, story writing, and role plays are all used to help the students explore and practice responses to abusive behaviors. Young people should be encouraged to let their abusive peers know how it makes them feel to be abused or to see someone else abused, and that they find the abusive behavior unacceptable.

Young people also need to learn how to continue to seek help if adults who are told of a juvenile's sexually abusive behavior minimize or dismiss the incident. Children and adolescents should be told that not all adults have had the opportunity to learn about sexual abuse committed by young people. In addition, they should be given resources, both in the school and the community, that will give them the needed help and support in dealing with juvenile sexual offending.

## Education for Adults

Parents, teachers, child care workers, and other adults who work with children or advise those who do need to be educated on the incidence and awareness of juvenile sexual offending. Equally important is the need to learn how to identify the differences between normal and abnormal sexual behaviors in children and how to respond appropriately to each.

Adults who routinely work with children usually have some knowledge of what is typical sexual behavior in children of a given age that often allows them to identify behaviors that are abnormal. However, adults must be reminded that not all common behaviors are healthy, acceptable, and nonabusive.

"Understanding and Responding to the Sexual Behavior of Children: A Perpetration Prevention Project" (Ryan et al., 1989) and the adult workshops of the Rhode Island Rape Crisis Center's "No More Abuse" program are training programs for adults that provide participants with information on and guidelines for distinguishing between normal and abnormal sexual behavior in children and adolescents. As discussed earlier, a systematic approach to evaluating the environment of the situation and the behavior will allow adults to categorize most observed or reported sexual behaviors as normal or abusive. It is important that workshops encourage adults to discuss with colleagues, specialists, and peers the sexual behaviors observed in young people. It is often easier to categorize a questionable behavior after some discussion. Because many adults are not comfortable discussing sexual behaviors, this process needs to be encouraged and supported by colleagues and professionals.

Once adults have learned how to categorize sexual behaviors, they need to learn how to respond to both the normal and the abusive behaviors. Normal sexual behaviors of juveniles should never be labeled as bad, dirty, prohibited, or subject to punishment. However, it is important to respond to normal sexual behaviors, especially if the adult walks in on the activity. When adults respond appropriately to normal behaviors, young people learn that their behaviors are normal and that the adult is available to discuss sexual behavior. An appropriate response to childhood sexuality should consist of labeling the behaviors observed and, if necessary, applying some boundaries for the behaviors. The response should not be judgmental and the behaviors should not be prohibited.

> An appropriate response to childhood sexuality should consist of labeling the behaviors observed and applying some boundaries for the behaviors.

If an adult discovers two young boys viewing and touching each other's private parts behind a tree on the playground, the adult might respond, "I see that you are exploring each other's penises. Penises are private parts of the body and are usually not shared on the playground. Is there a problem that I can help with?" By labeling the behavior, the adult demonstrates that he or she can discuss the sexual parts of the body and has educated the children on the use of correct terms for the sexual parts of the body. The adult does not tell the children that they are wrong for exploring, but lets them know that the playground is not the appropriate place for such exploration. An adult other than the primary caretaker(s) should not tell the children that the behavior would be acceptable in another setting because it could be confusing if the primary caretaker(s) set other limits on the children's sexual behavior. By asking if there is a problem, the adult lets the children know that they can ask questions and also gives the children the opportunity to provide additional information about the situation (such as an injury or the use of force or power in this or a previous situation). Labeling and limit setting should continue if the behavior is repeated. Regardless of how often the behavior is repeated, it should not be prohibited and the children should not be shamed or punished.

When educating adults on responding to normal sexual behavior, it should be remembered that many adults do not accept that any sexual behavior is normal and/or that they have had little or no experience in appropriately responding to normal childhood sexuality. Many adults will need continued support, encouragement, and feedback to learn to accept and respond appropriately to children's sexuality. I have found that just telling adults how to respond is usually not enough. It is important to allow people to ask questions, to practice and role-play appropriate responses, and to follow up with additional instructions and support.

When the observed or disclosed behavior is identified as abusive, a slightly different response is necessary. A sequence of responses to abusive sexual behavior by children has been developed by Ryan et al. (1989). When abusive sexual behavior is first discovered, it is important for the behavior to be labeled and for the young offender to be told that his or her behavior has a negative impact on those involved. The primary goal is for children to stop abusive behavior because they have learned that the behavior makes others feel bad, not because they will get into trouble if they do not. It is important to respond consistently to all types of abusive behaviors when they are first discovered, and not to wait to see if the situation escalates.

When sexual abuse committed by a child or adolescent is first discovered or disclosed, the typical response should be: "Karen told me that you were teasing her about her breasts. It makes me feel very uncomfortable that you were teasing Karen, and Karen told me it made her feel very angry." Notice, as with normal sexual behaviors, the response is not judgmental nor is the behavior prohibited or subject to punishment. The goal of this method is to give the children the opportunity to control their behaviors because of empathy, rather than the fear or threat of punishment. It should be acknowledged that it will be difficult for adults to not prohibit the behavior, but the point is to give the child the opportunity to learn to control his or her own behavior rather than to have adults control the child's behavior. After responding to the offender, the adult should speak with the victim or victims. Interaction with victims is very important so that the victims know that they did the right thing by telling and that the matter has been taken seriously. In speaking with the victim, several key elements of intervention are particularly important.

1. You should say that the victim is not responsible for the abuse and explore any guilt that the victim may have.
2. If the victim disclosed the abuse, let him or her know that you are glad he or she told.
3. The victim should know that you want to hear about any further problems, and you should explore any force that might have been used or may be used in the future to prevent the victim from telling.
4. Tell the victim what you are going to do about the situation. If you are not sure how you will respond until you speak with the offender, be sure to follow up by explaining your response to the victim.

After the initial disclosure, it is important to check with the victim to see if any further abuse has occurred. There is the possibility that the offender or others may make it difficult for the victim to disclose further abuse. If the victim has been physically injured, is scared or frightened, or if the offense is a crime, the parents or caretakers of the victim should be notified.

After an initial disclosure or discovery of juvenile offending, all adults involved with the offender should carefully monitor the offender and the situation in which the abuse occurred. The adults should watch carefully for signs that the offender is abusing again or is using force to keep victims or witnesses from disclosing. Someone should explore with the offender and the others involved their feelings about the abuse. After an abusive incident may be a natural time to educate children on sexuality, sexual abuse awareness and prevention, self-esteem, and communication skills. Remember that none of the lessons should imply directly or indirectly that a victim is ever responsible for abuse, or make any judgments about the children involved in the abuse.

Whenever abusive behavior is observed, adults need to consider reporting the incident to the local child protective services. The local laws concerning reporting of known or suspected child abuse or juvenile offending should always be followed. The recommendations described here deal only with adults' responses to juvenile offenders, and additional types of intervention may be required.

If the offender repeats the behavior or engages in a similar one, the second response should be the same: Label and react to the behavior and then confront the child and prohibit the behavior. The response must continue to be neither judgmental nor punitive: "Karen has told me that you were teasing her about her breasts again. I told you that teasing Karen makes me very uncomfortable and, according to Karen, it makes her angry. We have talked about this before. You need to stop teasing Karen." The child is told again that the behavior continues to affect those involved, but this time, the repeated behavior is prohibited by the adult because by repeating the behavior, the child has demonstrated an inability or unwillingness to control his or her behavior. Again, the adults involved need to speak to the victim about what happened and continue to monitor the offender and the situation.

If the sexually abusive behavior continues beyond the prohibition, Ryan et al. (1989) suggest that the previous response of labeling, describing the effect, confronting, and prohibiting be repeated and that the child be referred for evaluation.

If the abuse physically injures the victim, is a criminal offense, or for some other reason seems serious to the adults involved, it is appropriate to confront and prohibit the behavior and to refer the offender for evaluation even if the incident has been observed or reported only once. In these cases, the first response to the offender should still be the initial response of labeling the behavior and describing your feelings and, if you know them, the feelings of the victim. After some discussion with the offender, you can continue to respond to the incident by repeating the initial response and confronting and prohibiting the activity. If it seems appropriate, you might decide to refer the child for evaluation. Regardless of the seriousness of the activity and how far you wish to go with the intervention, the initial response must be simply labeling the behavior and describing your and the victim's feelings. If, after further discussion, the child volunteers to not repeat the behavior, accept the child's word and do not prohibit the activity—you may still decide to refer the child for an evaluation. Remember that the ultimate goal is to teach the offender empathy and to have the offender control his or her behaviors.

> *Remember that the ultimate goal is to teach the offender empathy and to have the offender control his or her behaviors.*

It is important that children who are developing abusive behaviors receive early intervention to prevent the development of abusive habits. Parents of a child who is abusing others may deny their child's behavior and/or blame the victim. An educated network of support staff is needed to deal seriously with children's inappropriate sexual activities and to support parents in seeking appropriate services for their child. Because many children who sexually abuse others have been sexually victimized themselves, it is important that repeat offenders be evaluated for sexual victimization. However, in those cases in which offenders are also victims, it is important that young offenders receive proper offender treatment and not just victimization treatment.

In the past decade, child sexual abuse prevention programs have focused on the prevention of victimization. Adult and child participants have been given an awareness of child sexual abuse issues and taught how to avoid victimization. Although such programs have been successful in preventing some child sexual abuse, it is now time to take a proactive approach to the prevention of child sexual abuse: the prevention of offending. With education and support, adults and young people will be able to identify young sexual abuse offenders, respond appropriately to the abusive behavior, and, when necessary, refer young people for early evaluation and treatment of offending behaviors.

# Monster Therapy

## *The Use of a Metaphor in Psychotherapy With Abuse Reactive Children*

**Sandra Ballester**

**Frederique Pierre**

Interest in the treatment of child sexual abuse has grown in the past few years. Still, there is very little literature that addresses actual methods of treatment for sexually abused children; even less has been written about children who become sexually abusive. As Waterman (1986) has noted, most of our knowledge about child sexual abuse originally came from case studies or through trial and error.

This chapter will address issues and approaches related to the treatment of abusive reactive children seen in a program designed especially for this population. For the purposes of this chapter, the term *abuse reactive* refers to children under the age of 13, most of whom have been sexually abused and who are now molesting other children.

The use of a "monster" metaphor will be discussed in addressing specific treatment issues. A step-by-step description of an effective strategy will include stages of treatment, aspects of the target population, and various treatment techniques and approaches used to engage these children. We will focus primarily on 6- to 8-year-olds, who have been the subject of this treatment approach for the past 6 years.

The increase in public awareness of the problem of child sexual abuse can be attributed to several factors. A surge of literature and media exposure came in the wake of several highly publicized cases involving the maltreatment of young children. Statistics maintained at local and national levels have also shown dramatic increases in the number of reported cases. More recently, the activism of adult survivors, including some in positions of high visibility, also have contributed to the increase in public concern about the victimization of children.

This heightened awareness, as well as increased public and private funding, contributed to an increase in the number of treatment programs established throughout the country to address the sexual abuse of children. Clinical research and experience in these programs over the past decade have taught or reaffirmed a variety of lessons about the problem. We have recognized that perpetrators of sexual abuse are not just adults or just males, but also adolescents and young children who have been referred for treatment because they have perpetrated sexually aggressive acts against other children. Also, data from clinical programs indicate that an increasingly high percentage of the victims seen in treatment is male (Rissin & Koss, 1987).

*Our understanding of the trauma caused by childhood victimization and its subsequent effects is just beginning to develop.*

Our understanding of the trauma caused by childhood victimization and its subsequent short- and long-term effects is just beginning to develop. Current literature relating to the effects of child sexual abuse indicates that most victims experience some type of reaction to the abuse situation (Conte & Berliner, 1988). Although clinical studies of long-term effects are sparse, we know that many chronic conditions have been attributed to childhood sexual abuse. Among these are phobias, regressive behaviors, somatic complaints, anger, guilt and shame-based personality disorders, sleep and eating disturbances, and sexual dysfunction. These can occur in varied degrees of frequency and duration (Berliner & Wheeler, 1987). Our knowledge of normal child development also teaches us that traumatization in the early stages of life can inhibit emotional development and adversely affect subsequent stages of development. The compensatory behaviors and world view that children develop in response to their abuse often contribute to maladaptive patterns later in life (MacFarlane, Cockriel, & Dugan, 1990). Although some research has suggested that certain aspects of a child's developmental status can offer some built-in protection from clinical disturbance, this is a relatively new theory that has not been thoroughly explored to date (Berliner & Wheeler, 1987).

Clearly, there is much to learn about the varied impact of childhood sexual abuse on later functioning, and about the seemingly wide range of reactions among otherwise similar individuals. Even more clear is the fact that we must pay more attention to the overt and the unconscious responses of child victims. The research of Conte and Berliner (1988), which found that 22% of the child victims of sexual abuse were asymptomatic at the time of intake, reminds us that symptoms are not the same as effects. Children react to, process, and integrate their victimization differently and in accordance with a wide array of variables. Their reactions may be obvious or they may be hidden—but experience has taught us that they are there. Reactions are sometimes transient, at other times persistent, and they often result in chronic problems that, without intervention, can last a lifetime.

Although we know even less about the effects of various interventions than we do about the effects of abuse, there is a clear shortage of specialized treatment programs geared to the developmental needs of specific populations of child victims. Because no empirical data exist to suggest which type of treatment is preferable in most cases, it is too soon to recommend a specific treatment (Berliner & Wheeler, 1987). Nevertheless, given the degree of unconscious or unseen responses to childhood abuse that may exist, we must move ahead with innovative methods of addressing the problems and effects that we are able to identify in children. This chapter addresses one such approach that, although still in an evolutionary stage, was developed in response to a problem that is becoming only too obvious.

## ■ The SPARK Program

Many clinicians, including ourselves, believe that early intervention is a crucial factor in our efforts to interrupt the cycle of abuse. Nowhere is this more apparent than in situations where abused children have begun to exploit or victimize children who are younger or more powerless than themselves. As a result, specialized treatment programs and specific therapeutic modalities are being developed to treat these sexually aggressive children who have been identified as abuse reactive. From this premise, the Support Program for Abuse Reactive Kids (SPARK) evolved and, from the experience gained there, the concept of monster therapy was developed. SPARK was established in January 1985 at Children's Institute International, a private, nonprofit, child abuse treatment agency in Los Angeles, California. The need for such a program was apparent to the program's founder, Kee MacFarlane, when she became aware of cases involving young children who were referred for treatment due to their age-inappropriate involvement in sexual activities with other children. Still in operation today, the SPARK program treats children ages 4 to 13 who have shown sexually aggressive behavior toward peers, siblings, and younger children in situations and/or relationships that are nonreciprocal or exploratory. (Further description of the origins of SPARK and other, similar programs can be found in *Newsweek* [March 30, 1992] or *Rolling Stone* [October 31, 1993].)

Group treatment, or peer group therapy, was chosen as the primary, though not exclusive, treatment modality because of its benefits in the areas of positive interpersonal relationships. In addition to specific clinical interventions, it also provides children with the opportunity to interact in a prosocial manner. It is cost-effective for low-income clients, it provides increased opportunities for supervision and support among clinical staff, and it is reportedly effective in the treatment of both adolescent perpetrators and youthful male victims of sexual abuse. Porter (1986) notes that the treatment modality is important because certain issues are prominent when addressing the problem of sexual abuse. Group therapy reduces the aspect of secrecy and provides an arena for members to explore their issues with a peer group that shares similar feelings and experiences.

In addition to group treatment for child clients, their parents or caretakers also are required to attend a parent group led by therapists in the SPARK program. These sessions are structured in a format parallel to the children's groups and are designed to help them address such issues as their child's and their own victimization, and reactions to the perpetration behavior. The parent group also serves as a forum where parents can obtain information about parenting problems and explore their attitudes about sex and sex education. The group further provides a means of support for parents who find themselves confronted by a wide array of feelings, such as anger and confusion. Parent conferences are held periodically to encourage parents to get further involved in their child's treatment. These sessions are beneficial because parents and therapists can exchange information and track the children's progress. A description of parent groups can be found in Chapter 7.

## The Metaphor of Monster Behavior

Monster therapy is a systematic, play therapy paradigm used to increase anger management, impulse control, self-esteem, and mastery in the sexually reactive child. It is an attempt to engage children in treatment and to facilitate their cognitive understanding of the group's lessons. Impulsive, sexual acting-out behavior is personified as monster behavior. It has been our experience that preadolescent boys latch on to the metaphor very quickly. They seem to enjoy a visual representation of their problem and realize that therapy can aid them in externalizing their problem. They see their problem (their monster), perhaps for the first time, as something outside of themselves that can be controlled and conquered. Monster therapy hopefully breaks the cycle in which acting out is the sum total of who they are as people or a constant reminder of all the things they've done wrong and felt powerless to stop. Monster behavior is also presented to the children as any behavior that gets them into trouble and is too hard to stop all by themselves. Thus children can see that there is a wide range of impulse control problems with which people (even adults) struggle, such as fighting, hurting people's feelings, drinking too much, eating too much, and so on. Pointing out the universality of impulse control problems often allows children to lessen some of their defenses and feel more bonded to the group.

Once the children identify with and understand the initial metaphor, they are introduced to the process of therapy. The process and stages of therapy are personified as a battle with the monster. This personification allows the therapists the opportunity to build their lesson plans and group activities around the monster theme.

All group activities, from the first session to the last, relate to conquering the monster. This consistent, integrated, and repetitive theme greatly increases the children's ability to learn new concepts. Thus monster therapy also can be described as a psychoeducational model.

It is important to note that from the beginning, the children are made aware that it is their impulsive *behavior* that is labeled and personified, not *them*. We never call children monsters. Because many of the boys we treat come into therapy externalizing responsibility for their problems, the ability to externalize and personify their impulse control problem as something outside of themselves has been an easy concept for them to grasp.

The idea of a monster was chosen because of the once-popular Saturday morning cartoon titled "My Pet Monster." My Pet Monster was a personified character that all the boys were familiar with and liked. The use of a monster for a personified impulse control problem also allowed the therapists the opportunity to refer to the problem of *having* monster behavior. The boys can see that although they may like the concept of monsters, monster behavior may not be something liked by others (i.e., parents).

# ■ Treatment Issues

In this section, we will attempt to identify the stages of treatment we have found to be effective in the treatment of this population. It is important to note that although we identify sex stages of treatment, we are not stating that children resolve all of their identified issues in each of the stages identified, just that the issues identified at each stage are the most salient. This model is fluid and all issues can run throughout treatment. The stages do not necessarily have a linear progression.

### Stage 1: Creating a Therapeutic Environment

#### *Building a Sturdy Fortress*

When sexually reactive boys first come to group therapy, they need a sense of protection. As summarized in Table 6.1, the therapeutic goal of the first stage of therapy is to provide a stable, safe, trusting environment where these children are free to explore their problems with little fear or shame. We hope to promote a cohesive group that allows for empathy development, increased social skills, and self-esteem. We hope to attain these goals by providing a formalized orientation and predictable group structure, and by working hard to make group fun.

To assess the child's feelings of safety and progress, we look for spontaneous disclosures of sexual reactivity problems from the child. The boys' formal orientation involves an introduction to the group's

**TABLE 6.1**  Stage 1: Creating a Therapeutic Environment

| *Primary Treatment Issues* | *Specific Discussion Topics* | *Treatment Goals* | *Graduation Criteria* |
|---|---|---|---|
| Self-esteem | Shame Guilt Assertiveness | Predictable structure to provide stability Safe environment to facilitate self-disclosure | Voluntary participation Exhibit understanding of basic group concepts, process, and structure |
| | | Promote group cohesiveness and trust | Take active role in initiating group process and/or in defining group structure |
| Trust | Secrecy Control Safety | Helping child separate problem behavior from self-image | Demonstrate ability to differentiate what they do from who they are |
| | | Engaging child in voluntary participation Making therapy a fun experience, not punishment | |
| Problem reframing | Monster metaphors | Reframe problem in terms of monster metaphor Identification of strengths and areas for improvement and self-esteem | |

rules and the token economy system. On the first day of group, each child is given his own small cup (i.e., monster cage) with his name printed clearly on the outside. This cup is a place for him to save all plastic animals (i.e., tokens) he will earn each week. Some groups make an activity of manufacturing monster cages out of Popsicle™ sticks instead of using cups (Diane Griggs, personal communications, 1989). We have a large box of assorted small plastic animals (monsters) that are used as tokens for appropriate behavior. When children demonstrate knowledge of a group rule or therapeutic concept, they immediately get to pick a plastic animal, or "monster," of their choice. When they have collected fifteen animals at the end of each group, they are allowed to exchange their animals for one of the many treats in the goody bag. The token economy is an ongoing reinforcement system. The children's cups are brought to every group and are kept on a special shelf in the therapist's office. It usually takes children 3 to 4 weeks to earn enough tokens for a toy car. We have found this economy system very effective not only in engaging the boys in the therapeutic process, but also allowing these impulsive children a visual means by which to assess their own progress. An additional goal of this system is to increase the children's self-esteem and sense of mastery. It is not uncommon to hear children saying, "Hey, I've got eleven animals" or "I can get four more today if I try hard." We find that when a child has worked hard for 3 weeks and has earned a toy car, his parents also have a means to gauge and reinforce his progress. It is important to note that children are rewarded for positive progress and that they are not rewarded for things that we would expect them to do intuitively (i.e., children are *never* rewarded for disclosures or for saying something supportive to other members).

### Predictable Environment

A formal orientation in group allows children to develop their own group rules, to discuss why they are in the group and how they feel about being there, and to obtain a description of the specific activities in which they will participate each week. We believe children need the sense of predictability and stability that formally orienting them to group therapy provides. A sense of predictability is always a vital component in developing trust and cohesion in the early stages of therapy. Because many of these children have not had consistent environments, predictability is the key to helping impulsive children manage their behavior. In addition to a formal orientation, we use a therapeutic "monster" metaphor throughout all six stages of treatment to increase the children's capacity to learn new skills and to increase the rate at which they learn.

> *A sense of predictability is always a vital component in developing trust and cohesion in the early stages of therapy.*

### Program Structure and Techniques

We believe that the formalized structure of the cognitive-behavioral groups themselves also can be a factor that promotes the child's emotional growth. This section will discuss specifically the components of formalized monster therapy group structure. This unique, cognitive-behavioral approach provides an overall structure that minimizes acting out within the group and allows the therapist as well as the child to assess weekly progress. Impulsive, sexually abused children have much difficulty staying on task and focusing on painful themes. Therefore, group structure is a necessity with this population. One of the most therapeutic components of monster therapy may be its consistency. The boys become accustomed to the repetitive structure, and the activities are integrated to the same theme. This stability and consistency does much to facilitate the boys' trust and cohesion. For example, it is not uncommon for long-time group members to be enthusiastic about teaching new group members the group rules, structure, token economy, and metaphor.

### Group Tools

To provide a safe environment for all children and to control any serious acting-out behavior that the children may display, time out is explained as part of a child's formal orientation. It is important to remember that the abuse reactive boys we treat have histories of severe aggression and manipulation of other children who are less vulnerable. To allow out-of-control (monster) behavior to continue in the group setting is a message that the behavior is acceptable and that the therapists are not able to contain such behavior. Children are told that if they are having a particularly rough day and are not able to keep their monsters in control, we will help them by separating them from the group until they are strong enough to get in control. We emphasize that we will not allow any group member to be hurt or any group rules to be chronically broken. The children are shown the corner in which they will sit for time out, and they are told the time limit. We try to reframe time out as an opportunity to get monster behavior in control. We also predict that at one time or another, they will probably need time out.

When new members first come to group, they fear how others will perceive them and what they will tell other group members about their "touching problem." This is often the most anxiety-provoking time for them because most were labeled "bad" once they were identified as reactive. The exercises that are used in this stage serve primarily as tools to enhance self-esteem, promote group cohesiveness, and reframe reactive behavior problems. To promote group cohesion, an exercise that we found to be very effective allows all members to actively participate in establishing group rules and allowing a group-generated "rule board" to outline what is expected from group members. For example, children take turns verbalizing an acceptable behavior in the group (e.g., no hitting, no touching). The role of the therapist is to help the children generate their rules by explaining the consequences of not adhering to group rules, and to also help the children understand that these rules are important to help keep *everyone* safe.

Thus the rules are equivalent to building a sturdy fortress in which behaviors that have created chronic problems can be contained within the group.

Another exercise that is used at this stage is titled "Ego Sandwiches." The goal of this exercise is to help children identify their strengths as well as problem areas. The therapists introduce the exercise as one in which the children will make a "special type of sandwich." The therapists tell the children that the sandwich is special, that they can't eat it, but they can feel good about it. The therapists bring in a plastic burger. We tell the children that the first piece of bread will represent something that they feel they do well, the meat represents something that they need to work on, and the last piece of bread represents something that they are proud of. Usually, children identify their "meat" as their touching problem. Others have identified problematic behaviors such as fighting or inappropriate expression of anger as their primary issues. Therapists may need to help children at some point understand how their anger and fighting may be tied into their reactivity issues. For example, one child in the group repeatedly shared his experience of getting angry at his caretaker, then victimizing younger children in the home as a result. Helping this child recognize his pattern of behavior promoted an understanding in the later stages of treatment regarding antecedents to his reactive behavior. The Ego Sandwich exercise is also useful for assessment. It can be used throughout the stages of treatment to assess any changes in children's self-esteem. This exercise may be difficult initially for the children. They may easily come up with negative things about themselves but be unable to identify any positive aspects. As treatment progresses and as self-esteem rises, this exercise is less difficult.

## Stage 2: Enhancing Self-Awareness

### Knowing Your Monster

The second stage of treatment in group (summarized in Table 6.2) is devoted to assessing the child's thoughts, feelings, and behavioral patterns of sexual reactivity. The children are encouraged to assess the antecedents of the problem, to assess their own arousal stimuli, and to discuss family dynamics that facilitate or perpetuate their acting out. Children are first encouraged to increase their ability to recognize general feelings. This is typically accomplished by using "feelings posters." Children are encouraged to define and expand their concepts of emotion. We instruct children to first focus on how their body is feeling in order to recognize "feeling cues" (e.g., anxiety or fear can feel like butterflies in your stomach; anger can make your face red, your head ache, your heart beat faster; sadness can feel like a lump in your throat, etc.). Children are also encouraged to use as many different emotions as possible and to recognize that they can feel more than one feeling at a time. Once this skill is achieved, the children progress to exploring the feelings experienced not only when they were victimized, but also later, when they victimized others.

Molested children are often fearful of expressing their own vulnerability and pain (especially boys who also molest others). In group, we structure a discussion of these painful topics and a role-play puppet show where characters also act out painful situations. The children are encouraged to model the puppet's attempts to talk about its feelings. Therapists facilitate the role plays with directed questions and statements such as "How must Mr. Bunny be feeling now?" "Has anyone else ever felt that way?" "Do you think we can be Mr. Bunny's friend and ask him to tell us how he's feeling now?" and "Look how happy Mr. Bunny feels now that he's talked to safe people."

For the most part, the sexually reactive boys in our monster groups have been victimized themselves. The therapist in the initial stages of treatment consciously works on exploring their feelings of shame, betrayal, homophobia, anger, and anxiety. Many activities and role plays are structured to explore these children's feelings.

**TABLE 6.2**  Stage 2: Enhancing Self-Awareness

| Primary Treatment Issues | Specific Discussion Topics | Treatment Goals | Graduation Criteria |
|---|---|---|---|
| Self-awareness | Identification of feelings Differentiation of affect | Identify and differentiate their feelings | Demonstrates desire to change behavior and deal with problem |
| | | Admit/accept that they have problems | Demonstrates desire to change behavior and deal with problem |
| Victimization | Disclosure Self-blame Homophobia Power and control | Recognize the antecedents to the problem (thoughts, circumstances, reinforcers, situations) | Provides a detailed picture of dynamics of his abusive behavior |
| | | Able to describe victimization experiences and his perceptions and feelings about them | Places appropriate blame |
| | | Identify situations that have high potential for sexual acting out | Verbalizes high-risk situations |
| Problem identification | Denial Cognitive distortion Responsibility Projection | | |
| Risk factors | Times Circumstances Behaviors Feelings | | |

Many role plays "reframe" feeling expression, disclosure, and empathy as powerful, strong activities. Much verbal reinforcement is given throughout group, and children often spontaneously demonstrate and/or model these behaviors. One specific role play often used is one in which the characters demonstrate nonabusive means of affection, and are aware of their own and sensitive to others' boundaries. These behaviors are depicted as safe, strong, smart, and a way to be a good friend. Children are also encouraged to teach the characters how to be assertive about their need for appropriate boundaries (e.g., "Bobby, can you show Mr. Bunny how to tell Mr. Cow that he doesn't like to be hugged without permission?" and "How could Mr. Cow *ask* for a hug?"). These boys are encouraged to reframe their often-distorted perceptions of peer, control, affection, sex, and gender roles through puppet shows and role plays. They are then reinforced for empathy, nurturance, problem solving, and cooperative behaviors. We spend much time in this stage reeducating children about power, control, and responsibility. To allow for a greater sense of mastery and self-esteem, children in the later stages of treatment are encouraged to take a more active teaching role in group. For example, when a child has completed homework assignments and has not had a sexual acting-out incident for a month, he is allowed to be in charge of handing out animal tokens in the group. It is believed that these special privileges also help children assess their own progress. The member of the group that has the most seniority is also appointed to explain group rules, time out, and other concepts to new group members. It has been our experience that children derive much satisfaction and self-esteem when they have conquered their monster enough to teach others.

## Stage 3: Learning Alternative Behaviors and Skills

### *Planning for Battle*

In this stage, the children identify strategies for battling their monsters. The focus is on problem-solving and cognitive skills for impulse control (see Table 6.3). Anger is a major emotion for most of the sexually reactive boys with whom we work. These children have a very difficult time recognizing any possible emotions, such as frustration or hurt. Anger is a very powerful emotion for them. It is our job to encourage expression of emotion by prosocial means (e.g., increasing assertive behaviors) and to reframe a destructive anger response as "out of control" or as monster behavior. We attempt to break the impulsive response pattern by teaching children how *powerful* it is to be in control and appropriately assertive. We want them to see that prosocial behaviors decrease the likelihood that the anger-creating situations will occur in the future. We also explore if there is a well-developed pattern of anger leading to sexual arousal in these children. Most of these children

**TABLE 6.3**  Stage 3: Learning Alternative Behaviors and Skills

| Primary Treatment Issues | Specific Discussion Topics | Treatment Goals | Graduation Criteria |
|---|---|---|---|
| Impulse control | Cognitive restructuring Self-talk techniques High-risk strategies | To frame distortions and rationale regarding abusive behavior<br><br>To identify ways to avoid high-risk situations To develop alternative behavior strategies | Child displays appropriate problem-solving abilities Demonstrates ability to control behavior in group |
| Social skills | Nonabusive affection Intimacy Appropriate socialization Managing anger and anxiety Communication skills | To communicate needs and feelings to others<br><br>To interact appropriately<br><br>To differentiate sexual/nonsexual touching | Child manages anger, frustration, and anxiety in an acceptable way Communicates needs appropriately Respectful interaction with group members |
| Empathy | Power/ powerless Identifying others' feelings Benefits of helping others Scapegoating | To model empathetic behavior and reinforce helping behavior<br><br>To increase intrinsic reinforcement | Child recognizes impact of behavior and statements on others Able to reinforce others for positive social behavior Child can correctly verbalize feelings of others |
| Sex education | Sexual myths/facts Sex role stereotyping Androgeny | To convey factual information about sex<br><br>To broaden concepts of gender-specific behavior | Child possesses accurate information |

do not know that there are other ways to express their anger that are effective, prosocial, and nonviolent.

In organizing a plan of attack for these children, the monster metaphor becomes very important. Self-talk, thought stopping, and thought shifting are all taught. One example is that the children read the group's "monster book" and practice self-talk ("I can control myself if I really try") to make the monsters go away. Relaxation and stress-management exercises such as deep-breathing techniques are also taught at this stage. The main goals of Stage 3 are to help the children develop new ways to deal with anger, guilt, loss, anxiety, and sexual arousal; to develop a course of action for high-risk situations; and to teach children ways to quickly assess and avoid high-risk situations. The main therapeutic goal is for children to combine skills in a way that helps them develop an internalized locus of control. We want children to learn to interrupt the arousal impulsive patterns they have developed and to replace these patterns with new thoughts and skills.

*Children who are sexually reactive chronically find themselves in trouble without much clue as to how they got there.*

Children who are sexually reactive chronically find themselves in trouble without much clue as to how they got there and with even less understanding of how to change their behavior. The common responses from the boys treated in our program, when asked at intake why they molested, are "It felt good," "They made me," and "I don't know." Our job as clinicians is not only to help the child answer these questions for himself but to also provide him with skills to effectively address therapeutic issues.

In our group, impulse control is defined as a recognition of alternative behavioral strategies and effective problem solving. Children must be able to interrupt their identified impulsive arousal patterns with self-talk and to follow through with their individualized control strategy. The problem-solving (impulse control) strategy proposed in monster therapy was introduced by Spivack and Shure (1974). This teaching strategy has proven successful as a preventive measure for both well-adjusted and poorly adjusted children. When confronting a troubling situation, children in group are encouraged to (a) identify the problem; (b) generate behavioral options (such as talk with a trusted adult, self-talk, or removing oneself from the situation and doing something else); (c) predict the consequences; (d) choose and apply a solution to the identified behavior; and (e) evaluate and change the behavior if needed (they ask themselves and the group, "Did my plan work?") (Committee for Children, 1988).

According to Committee for Children (1988), an important way to increase a child's ability to control his behavior is to teach verbal *mediation*; in other words, to require the children to problem solve aloud. According to Camp and Bash (1975), cognitive performance, discrimination learning, and the ability to control motor behavior increase with verbal self-instruction with children. Our experience with these children has taught us that *repetitive* verbal mediation enhances the process of breaking a problem into its small (conquerable) parts. A group structure that strongly emphasizes positive verbal reinforcement, self-reinforcement, and peer reinforcement is also important. Interestingly, Braswell and Kendall (1985) concluded that statements of encouragement (e.g., "Keep up the good work," "I can see you're really trying hard") were associated with more positive child behavioral changes, whereas simple confirming statements (e.g., "That's correct" and "Right") were not. It is important to remember that it is the rare child who will come into the group intrinsically motivated to learn new behaviors because it will make his life richer. Children usually come to therapy because someone else has a problem with their behavior. To motivate the latency-aged child to make changes, the therapist needs to tap the child's sense of mastery and pride. In this stage, children are encouraged to talk about what they have been told or what they think about sex in general. We often spend the majority of these sessions confronting sexual myths and stereotypes ("boys can't cry," "to be sensitive means you're gay"). We also encourage anger expression in group and at home (i.e., talking about feelings) and conflict resolution.

To increase a child's self-esteem, we encourage many activities to allow children mastery experiences. Successes as well as attempts at successes are reinforced in the group. Once the child has mastered a concept and it has been reinforced, we hope that the experience increases the positive qualities he sees in himself. In order for these children to be motivated to learn nonabusive means of meeting their needs, they must first feel positive about themselves. Once sexually reactive children begin to believe they are not horrible and uncontrollable, they may be able to work on developing a sense of empathy.

> Empathy is a key ingredient in developing pro-social behaviors and interpersonal problem solving skills. Without the ability to perceive, predict, and identify with another's feelings, children may learn a problem solving model, but make decisions which only benefit themselves. (Committee for Children, 1988, p. 10)

Our goal is to promote increased social skills by means of empathy training. Most of our problem-solving role plays require children to put themselves in others' shoes. For example, many of our monster puppets often act out high-risk situations that have gotten the better of them. The children are encouraged to teach the puppets new self-talk and techniques to interrupt the monsters' patterns of behavior. The children often identify with the puppets and have no problem encouraging the puppets to "try harder, think about it different" (cognitive restructuring), "concentrate more," and to "think of what will happen if you don't get in control." We also hear children make encouraging and positive reinforcement statements to the monster puppets.

### Stage 4: Identifying and Using Resources

#### *Rallying Your Forces*

The goals of Stage 4 are to engage the parents and family in the treatment process (see Table 6.4). It is vital that the parents are the child's allies. The parents need to understand the premise and activities (e.g., homework assignments) of monster therapy and to be encouraged to reinforce and track progress at home and at school. At the same time, children need to be encouraged to share, trust, and disclose to parents, and to elicit their parents' help, especially in high-risk times. In this stage, the therapist helps the boys generalize new skills, and the behaviors are implemented at home and at school. Parents are actively engaged in this process by monitoring homework assignments. The goal is to create a "safe fortress" with one or both parents so that the boys can go to a parent when they feel at risk of sexually acting out. There are several ways in which we accomplish the goals outlined in this stage. Parallel treatment in this stage is crucial; there needs to be frequent communication between the therapist and the parents. Through parent conferences and in parent groups, parents are given specific ways in which they can help their children in high-risk situations. In cases where parents were not well informed, they tended to react to their children's disclosures about high-risk situations and/or wanting to act out by using inappropriate or very punitive responses. For example, in the early years of the program, we had not adequately prepared parents to deal with their children's need to seek them out at high-risk times. One child expressed to his parents that preparing to

**TABLE 6.4** Stage 4: Identifying and Using Resources

| Primary Treatment Issues | Specific Discussion Topics | Treatment Goals | Graduation Criteria |
|---|---|---|---|
| Resource identification | Trustworthiness Resource availability | To recognize components of trustworthiness | Child is able to identify a network of resources |
| | Prioritize support systems | To increase child's ability to identify available resources | Verbalizes plan to use resources |
| | | To reframe requests for help as a strength | Demonstrates ability to prioritize use of resources |
| Assertiveness skills | Positive self-concept Asking for help | To develop action plans, priorities, and resources | Displays ability to tolerate frustration |
| | Using resources | To broaden concepts of gender-specific behavior | Takes active role in problem-solving exercises |
| Problem solving | Needs vs. wants Strategy formulation Using resources | | |

take a bath with his younger sibling sexually stimulated him. The parental response was to slap him and send him to his room.

Another way in which we help children identify resources is through role playing difficult situations. The therapists write out situations on 3×5 cards in which children as a group not only problem solve situations but develop a list of people on whom they could call to help the characters in the role play. In the second part of the exercise, children prepare individual lists that can be used outside of group. The therapists help children develop a broad list so that they have many people to contact. We explain to children that in life, we must plan for many types of difficult situations (e.g., fires, earthquakes, etc.). We further explain that we do not wait for those dangerous situations to occur before developing a plan.

We encourage children to report what was effective and what was ineffective. Depending on the report, we may revise the plan until it is workable for the child. One child in the group had an experience in which his plan was tested. He began to feel sexually stimulated at school and decided to put his plan in action. Although we had gone to great lengths to notify his teachers about his plan, on that particular day he had a substitute teacher, who was not aware of his need to make contact. His effort to explain his situation to her proved futile, so he asked to go to the principal's office and called his parents, who were not home. The child continued his attempts to use all resources and finally obtained permission from an administrator to beep us.

The plan at this stage is to have children generalize their problem-solving skills with respect to high-risk situations outside the group to other areas of their lives, such as home and school.

### Stage 5: Putting Skills Into Practice

#### Conquering the Monster

In this stage, the goal is to have the boys internalize their locus of control (see Table 6.5). We hope that by this stage, cognitive mastery of the skills has occurred, and the goal is to practice new skills in as many situations as possible. The boys try their new skills over and over to determine what works and what does not. They learn to adapt and to change. For instance, many boys learn to approach an alternate person for help if their parents are unavailable.

For these boys, conquering the monster means taking responsibility for their own actions—realizing the problem *within* themselves and conquering it *within* themselves. Internalizing a sense of control is a key concept to monster control. In the initial stages, we facilitate the children's image of the problem as a monster, out there somewhere, that makes them act out, but as therapy progresses, we consciously switch both the discussions and the focus from the monster behaviors to their thoughts and reactions. Children are encouraged to look at the progress they have made.

> *For these boys, conquering the monster means taking responsibility for their own actions.*

In this stage and throughout the therapy process, we structure homework assignments, role plays, and various opportunities for peer and therapist modeling of appropriate behaviors. Homework assignments allow children the opportunity to practice their newly acquired, *learned*

**TABLE 6.5**  Stage 5: Putting Skills Into Practice

| Primary Treatment Issues | Specific Discussion Topics | Treatment Goals | Graduation Criteria |
|---|---|---|---|
| Empowerment | Self-esteem/ confidence | To enhance feelings of competence by reinforcement | Child demonstrates successful problem-solving strategies |
| Locus of control | Responsibility Self-control | To improve child's communication skills | Child displays decreased reliance on external controls |
| Internalizing skills | Elements of mastery | To increase child's tolerance for frustration | Increase in positive self-control Assists others with problem solving |

skills in their home and school environments. Most homework assignments require the children to bring their assignments back to group for discussion. An example of a homework assignment is instructing the child to practice telling his mother when he feels like sexually acting out, or instructing him to identify for his mother and father which situations and/or activities lead to high-risk times at home. For homework assignments to be effective and for a child's skills to be generalized to different settings, the child's parents must be actively involved in his treatment plan. They must be educated regarding the metaphor of controlling the monster, and also therapeutically engaged in order to reinforce and monitor the child's progress at home and at school. Frequent parent conferences and updates in the middle stages of treatment are therefore necessary. Once the child has not acted out sexually for 6 to 9 months, he is encouraged to take more of a group teacher role. As these children teach others to stop, think, plan, and ask for help in high-risk times, it is not surprising that their skills become ingrained and control becomes more internalized.

Children are also encouraged to bring reports of relapse back to group so that we can determine what went wrong. Relapse prevention is a main focus of the group. The boys identify problems that could possibly cause them to act out sexually again, and the therapist works hard

**TABLE 6.6**  Stage 6: Skill Mastery and Relapse Prevention

| Primary Treatment Issues | Specific Discussion Topics | Treatment Goals | Graduation Criteria |
|---|---|---|---|
| Generalizing skills to other situations | Application of skills/concepts | Able to apply concepts to other feelings and behaviors (anger, stress, etc.) | Child demonstrates mastery of clinical concepts and behavior skills |
| Applying concepts learned | Prediction of problem to different problem situations | Able to predict potential problems when formulating action plans | Demonstrates ability to project solutions for theoretical situations |
| Relapse prevention | Potential for relapse Prediction of behavior | To recognize that relapse potential always exists | Has a plan for appropriate course of action if relapse occurs |
| | Black/white thinking Disclosure/ self-tolerance | Able to revise thinking, planning, and actions | Displays flexibility and self-tolerance under pressure |

to lower the guilt for the sexual behaviors so that, should a relapse occur, it will not overwhelm the child. The boys are taught to stop blaming others and to concentrate on solving the problem.

## Stage 6: Termination and Relapse Prevention

### Becoming a Knight

The final way in which we structure the group to allow predictability, and to integrate new skill learning, is by ceremonializing termination (see Table 6.6). When a child has made the progress necessary to enable him to terminate his group therapy, the group members prepare for the child's termination party. We call this ceremony "knighthood." This is a time when a child has consistently demonstrated in group therapy, at home, in school, and with friends his ability to control his monster. He has been able to control his sexual acting-out behavior and has mastered the skills that prove a higher self-esteem. All members talk of this child's accomplishments, their feelings at losing a group member, and then formally say goodbye. In front of his parents and other peers, the terminating child is presented with a certificate of knighthood (i.e., achievement). We make every effort to make this the knight's finest hour. All the wonderful advantages of being a knight are bestowed on him. There is a ceremony for termination in which the boy receives a cape and a scroll, and he is presented as a knight to the parents' group that meets at the same time as the children's group. As a knight, the boy is given the responsibility of recognizing monster warning signs. He is expected to know that the monster may return and that the knight may need help to conquer the monster again.

On termination from the group, children are encouraged to use the relapse problem-solving skills learned outside of group. They are also encouraged to assess the resources available to them for such an endeavor.

## ■ Conclusion

Monster therapy not only provides the abuse reactive child with an externalized visual and consistent theme, but also engages him in the therapeutic process. Although monster therapy is a relatively new therapeutic intervention, it is one that has attempted not only to promote a sense of mastery in the sexually reactive child, but also to allow a framework that takes into consideration the child's developmental level. Professionals in the field may find this paradigm beneficial as well as useful in expanding their own clinical work with this population.

# 7

# Parallel Treatment of Parents of Abuse Reactive Children

Diane R. Griggs

Armond Boldi

When perusing the literature regarding child sexual abuse (still a relatively new field), the majority of information is on the victimization of children. Needless to say, it is very difficult to find literature on the treatment of parents and caretakers of children who molest. Parents are an integral part of the children's treatment plan and vital to a healthy prognosis, yet they are a forgotten population.

Similarly, as the literature and current publications (*Newsweek*, March 30, 1992, and *Rolling Stone*, October 31, 1992) negate the importance of parent treatment by omitting quality reference to this population, it is sad to say that many colleagues do just the same. Therapists vie for the chance to work with child victims and child victimizers but feel cheated or put upon when asked to work with parents. It seems that parents just don't hold the same curiosity and/or notoriety. However, without the parents' participation, there would be no children in treatment. Parents' participation can bring successful treatment or sabotage it.

This chapter will focus on treating the parent and caretaker of the abuse reactive child. For our purposes, the word *parent* will be used synonymously for caretaker unless otherwise specified. The basis of the information provided is from our experience as the parent group therapists of the Support Program for Abuse Reactive Kids (SPARK) at Children's Institute International—a private, nonprofit child abuse treatment agency in Los Angeles, California—and a role that the senior author assumed a few months after the inception of SPARK. She had been running the parents' group for 10 years.

# ■ General Program Description

## Membership

Parental participation is mandatory for acceptance into the program because the home environment is crucial for diminishing the reactive behavior. The parents of children who are reactive come from dysfunctional, multiproblem families of origin. Approximately 80% have a history of having been sexually or physically abused (Johnson, 1988). Group treatment is the treatment of choice, although adjunct modalities are also available depending on the family's needs. Via the group treatment experience, the parents become hopeful for change.

According to Yalom (1985), the instillation of hope is the most important curative factor because it promotes willingness to return to treatment so that the other curative factors can take effect. Parents who are in the beginning stages need to know that they are not the only ones with this horrifying problem; Yalom (1985) calls this universality. These two factors are extremely important because they allow the parents to get "hooked" into treatment, normalize their fears and self-blaming perceptions, and combat the isolation caused by humiliating feelings. During her first session, upon hearing the stories of the other parents, one young mother exclaimed, "Now I don't feel so bad." A "veteran" parent stated, "This is the only time I can talk to adults." This parent was so vigilant about protecting her children that she isolated herself and her young children.

The group has been composed of single mothers, two-parent families, gay couples, foster parents, adoptive parents, and alternative caretakers (e.g., group home caregivers). The socioeconomic and educational levels can vary widely within the group, and the racial composition is heterogeneous, with black and Hispanic members forming the majority. Group members often develop alliances and engage socially outside of the group.

Many families are monitored by Child Protective Services (CPS) or the County Department of Probation. CPS or probation involvement is welcomed by the therapists for two reasons. First, these systems are a deterrent for premature termination because they provide specific goals and guidelines that motivate participation and assist the families in controlling and supervising reactive behaviors. Second, both parents and reactive children realize that there is a debt to pay to society via community service, confinement, or probation. The seriousness of the behavior—whether it is fondling, exhibitionism, digital penetration, or sodomy—is communicated to the families.

### Leadership

Leadership is composed of a male-female cotherapeutic team that provides support, education, and therapeutic intervention. The team assists parents with the resolution of their own victimization issues, strengthens the parent/child relationship, and provides child sexual abuse education and human sexuality education (Johnson, 1988).

### Program Structure

The group runs in 14-week cycles. There is generally a cycle break of approximately 2 to 4 weeks around a holiday period. During this time, new assessments are completed for families who will begin the following cycle and current families can continue with adjunct services. The parents' group meets concurrently with the children's group. Parents are encouraged to develop relationships with their children's therapists and to share information as often as possible. Prior to the end of the 14-week cycle, parents and children meet with the children's therapists to discuss progress and treatment goals. There is a social event prior to each cycle's end. Pre- and postsupervision is attended by all therapists where case management issues, clinical issues, and clinical interventions are reviewed and countertransference issues are explored.

## ■ Goals of Treatment

There are two goals of treatment. The first is to strengthen the family unit by focusing on healthier interactional communication patterns; the second is to decrease the pathology by creating healthier family dynamics, thus ensuring that the family is a safe place for the victim and/or the reactive child. In many family units, the victim and the reactive child live in the same home. These goals can be accomplished by incorporating the following ten objectives.

> Parents entering treatment often feel powerless as they deal with systems that suddenly have control over their lives.

*Empower parents so they can negotiate within the legal, law enforcement, CPS, school, and child care systems.* When parents enter treatment, they often feel powerless as they deal with systems that suddenly have control over their lives. Parents struggling with their own anxieties don't assert personal rights in these various areas. Education about the systems as well as anticipatory guidance about court processes empowers parents to become active and nonreactive when dealing with the systems.

*Provide child sexual abuse education.* Most of the parents are unaware of the dynamics of sexual abuse and abuse reactive children. Much time is spent educating parents in this area. Parents learn to identify abuse-specific emotional themes, issues, and behaviors. This new knowledge helps the parents to be more supportive of their children and augments their ability to provide appropriate parenting interventions. Initially, a parent may punish the child who wets the bed, but when the behavior is reframed, the parent can assist in managing the child's behavior, thus contributing to a healthy recovery. Healthy communication in the family about sexuality is encouraged.

*Assist parents with supervision of the reactive child and the victim.* An important goal is to protect the victim. Parents may fail to recognize or may minimize the importance of supervising the reactive child; for example, bathing, toileting, and sleeping routines are often overlooked as high-risk situations. Although some parents feel as if they are policing their children, parents can be quite creative around supervision issues. Several parents have talked about strategically placing mirrors in the home so they can keep an eye on their children. Others are hypervigilant for silences. After some time, this new behavior becomes automatic. Ideally, parents learn to safeguard the children's environment until the children learn to develop internal controls to prevent additional reactivity.

*Provide general child development information.* Most parents are not aware of the developmental tasks and needs of their children. Education of developmental stages enables the parents to better understand their children and to help work through issues in each stage of development. Education provides a baseline so parents can identify problem areas.

*Provide general sexual development information and distinguish between normal versus reactive behavior.* Most parents of reactive children are overly concerned with any sign of sexuality in their children. Therapists help parents to recognize age-appropriate sexual behaviors. Knowledge of normal development helps to diminish parents' anxiety and enables them to identify if intervention is necessary.

*Help parents develop insight into family dynamics and recognize how these dynamics contribute to the manifestation of reactive behaviors.* Parents learn how their own families of origin and current family dynamics contribute to their children's reactive behaviors. By reexamining their belief systems, sexual behaviors, and attitudes, parents can identify what "baggage" they bring to their own parenting experience. Appropriate perceptions and behaviors are adopted. This experience gives them a sense of control over their own lives and a realistic view of their children's future.

*Assist parents with parenting skills and behavior management issues.* As children, many of the parents lacked appropriate parent figures and/or guidance in their lives. Therefore, therapists model parenting as well as teach parenting skills using cognitive, behavioral interventions. The reactive child is already quite familiar with the reactive behavioral approach because it is included in the monster paradigm (see Chapter 6 by Ballester and Pierre, this volume), and this approach can be easily transitioned into the home. This helps parents to teach delayed gratification and helps their children to diminish their reactivity.

*Assist parents in normalizing fears, shame, and humiliation.* Parents are encouraged to talk about their shame, guilt, fears, and humiliation. With the support of the group leaders and group members, parents learn to accept, rather than avoid, their feelings. This process helps the group members to normalize their feelings to develop healthier self-concepts.

*Strengthen support system and resources.* Many of the parents have chosen to isolate themselves socially or to terminate careers, schooling, and so on as a result of their crises. They do not use or trust the resources in their community because it is these same community resources where many of their children were victimized. Parents can begin to build their own support system through exchanging their personal experiences. Parents on their own can initiate contact outside of the group so they can assist fellow members when in need. After rebuilding their trust, parents begin to use community resources as they feel more empowered working with various systems.

*Assist in the development of appropriate expectations of treatment goals.* One of the biggest disappointments that the parents face is the continuation of reactive behavior and/or related symptomology (e.g., bed wetting, masturbation). Parents enter treatment seeking a cure, but instead must learn to have realistic expectations of themselves and their children. Progress is not necessarily a linear process; it is often more similar to a roller coaster ride. Parents tend to develop a false sense of security during the "highs" and despair during the "lows." Eventually, parents learn to reinforce their children when they start to make progress.

## ■ Treatment Issues and Themes

There are initial issues that need immediate attention because parents have mixed emotions toward their reactive children regarding the perpetration behavior (Johnson, 1988). For parents, the perpetration behavior elicits an intense amount of emotion and confusion. They develop a love-hate dynamic toward their reactive children and may withdraw emotionally and physically. This behavior reinforces the "I'm bad" syndrome discussed in this volume by Ballester and Pierre (Chapter 6). Parents may blame themselves and feel that they were directly responsible for the abuse reactive behavior.

*Parents may blame themselves and feel that they were directly responsible for the abuse reactive behavior.*

Anger toward the child and self often turns into anger toward the system.

If not handled appropriately, this displaced anger can later become a factor preventing the parents from working through their emotional issues. It is important to realize that a certain amount of anger will always remain and that the treatment focus should be to redirect it and to decrease the intensity so that the anger becomes manageable. As the group progresses, other issues and themes manifest, some of which we discuss below.

*Preoccupation with and the minimization of abuse reactive behaviors.* Parents usually have legitimate questions and concerns about their children's reactive behavior. However, feelings of shame, guilt, fear, and anger can become so intolerable that parents must find a respite from those feelings, and do so by projecting their feelings onto their reactive children. Specifically, some parents minimize the seriousness of the reactive behavior, are preoccupied with the need to know all the details of the abuse situation, or identify their children only as victims. This behavior is a cue to therapists that the parents may be in denial about their children's behaviors.

*Personal levels of anxiety and stress.* In addition to the daily stress, the parents are faced with additional anxiety specific to their situations. These pressures include involvement with courts and CPS; supervision of their reactive children; anxiety caused by their children's continuing symptoms related to their reactive behavior at home and in public places (e.g., schools); their feelings about the process of recovery from their own abuse histories; and having to participate in treatment.

All of these pressures can cause the parents to become abusive, isolated, depressed, and/or emotionally withdrawn, and they can lead to adjustment difficulties (e.g., divorce, substance abuse).

*Good/bad parent issues.* One of the issues encountered in the parents' group is the self-perception that parents are either "good" or "bad." The "good" parents are unwilling to take responsibility for their reactive children. These parents are minimally open to suggestion and receiving information.

The "bad" parents, on the other hand, feel totally defeated and hopeless, and will give up their parenting responsibilities to the treatment team and other systems. In both cases, these parents need to be monitored in terms of supervising their reactive children. For example, one young mother, fearing her inability to parent, gradually withdrew from her role as a parent and forfeited the parenting responsibility to our treatment team. Her child became more anxious and angry toward this parent and transferred the good parent role to the primary group therapist. Parents can also perceive themselves as "victims" and engage in self-pitying behaviors.

*Need for details of disclosure incident.* Some parents, especially at the beginning of their treatment, tend to be overly interested in knowing the details of sexual reactivity. Our experience is that this need for detail is used by the parents to minimize their feelings of guilt and shame. The children feel threatened when the parents are overly concerned and any positive interactional communication patterns are at risk, promoting secret keeping.

*Cultural and religious issues.* Parents can use culture and religion to cope with the anxiety of managing abuse reactive behaviors and to deal with distressing sexual issues. Some find refuge in their religious teachings and sayings heard in childhood, often citing Scripture or cultural myths, such as "masturbation will cause blindness." At times, parents are so rigid in their thinking that they cannot entertain information to the contrary. Distressing sexual behaviors should be reframed so parents understand that the behaviors have purpose. For example, the parent who views masturbation as "bad" can understand that this behavior can be self-soothing or it can be a sign of anxiety. Thus the behavior can be tolerated with reason (e.g., in the privacy of the child's room).

*Personal, unresolved abuse issues.* Parents may have their own unresolved victimization issues that may prevent them from accomplishing treatment goals. They may project their own issues onto their children.

"Gertrude" has nine siblings who all have perpetration and/or victimization issues. Gertrude's father is the identified perpetrator of several of Gertrude's siblings, but Gertrude denies any victimization history although personal content, behavior, and history suggest otherwise. Gertrude has 7 children, 4 of whom are reactive and have victimization histories. The other 3 have only victimization histories identified. Gertrude describes her oldest girl, age 9 (who is reactive and is an identified victim who has multiple victimizations), as a child on the prowl, looking for sexual encounters.

Gertrude cannot empathize with this child who "keeps getting herself molested." Because Gertrude has not resolved her own victimization, she cannot assist her child. However, she can be somewhat empathetic and can provide adequate supervision for her sons and her youngest daughter.

*Setting up the reactive child to reoffend.* The family dynamics can contribute to the resurfacing of abuse reactive behaviors. Parents who are lenient with supervision, present confused sexual messages, or recreate the initial abuse dynamics can foster new reactive behaviors.

"D.J.," who is 8 years old, was asked to bathe one of his younger siblings after his mother had just scolded him for not doing his chores. He reluctantly did as he was told, feeling angry and humiliated. A short time later, his mother entered the bathroom to find D.J. orally copulating with his younger brother.

In cases like this, protective systems can provide appropriate external controls (e.g., probation, detention, and supervision for the family).

*Sexuality.* Parents who struggle with their own sexuality issues often behave in ways that stimulate their reactive children's sexual impulses. Mothers can dress seductively, and parents can present overwhelming sexual climates. For example, one family that contained both the victim and the reactive child regularly ate dinner in the nude. This behavior definitely put the family at risk.

*Family secrets.* Families often have secrets that keep the unhealthy dynamics alive. There may be a silent or overt message to remain silent about relationships or about supervision issues such as sleeping arrangements, visitation, and recurrences of reactive behavior. Parents may be silent about ongoing issues, but the children often are the family historians and will reveal the intimacies.

## ■ The Group Treatment Modality

As mentioned previously, the treatment of choice is group treatment. However, before a family can be admitted into the program, it must first complete an assessment. Many times, some of the family members, including the reactive child, may not be group appropriate and may need to begin treatment via another modality. The whole family must complete an intake processs so that their group readiness can be assessed. SPARK consists of several perpetrator groups, the parent group, a sibling treatment group, and a victim group for those children whose siblings are being treated in the perpetrator group.

## Staffing and Supervision

The SPARK staffing and supervision clinical team consists of professional volunteers, interns, and postdoctoral candidates, all of whom have a variety of experience. The SPARK staff is primarily responsible for supervision, providing intervention techniques and theory for practice. Each group is led by a cotherapeutic team, preferably a male/female team. The primary therapist is a licensed clinician who has experience working with this population. The cotherapist can be a professional volunteer or a student intern. Prior to the group, the program staff meets for presupervision to discuss case management and clinical issues, and time is allotted for the cotherapist teams to meet to discuss group plans. After group, a debriefing or postsupervision is held to discuss group themes and individual issues, including risk assessment (e.g., child abuse reporting), and to provide an arena for therapists to unload and process countertransference and anxiety-related issues.

The debriefing process is extremely important because this therapeutic work can be quite draining and can elicit a variety of feelings and countertransferences. The clinician often feels ineffective, frustrated, and overwhelmed; in fact, the supervision experience can parallel the process of the treatment groups. It is important that the clinician get positive feedback and nurturance from the supervision group. To foster this, at the end of each cycle, a social is organized to honor and praise the clinical team.

## Assessment

The assessment team is composed of the SPARK staff and meets to discuss case management issues prior to interviewing the family. These issues include: (a) the identification of family members, including the victim, siblings with reportedly no abuse histories, and reactive children; (b) the discussion of disclosure information, including who made the disclosure, to whom the disclosure was made, the nature of disclosure, and any accompanying documentation (e.g., medical exam, police report); (c) the current status of the reactive children (e.g., system involvement, current living arrangements); (d) high-risk issues (e.g., victims and reactive children living within the same home, family dysfunction, such as the parents' own abuse history); and (e) child care history.

It is important to interview everyone in the family separately during the intake in order to assess other potential victims and to reveal family secrets. It is surprising to find out what siblings can reveal. Parents may feel that siblings who have been unexposed to information about the abuse have nothing to contribute to the assessment. However, these siblings often are the family historians and know more about the abuse than their parents believe. While conducting three separate interviews of a family that included a mother and two siblings, the mother clearly stated in response to direct questions that she wasn't aware of any abuse in her home and that the victims never attempted to disclose to her. On completion of the separate interviews, however, the clinician who interviewed the victims reported that both of them attempted to disclose to their mother. The mother confronted the perpetrator, who denied the allegations, and, as a result, the mother warned the victims to never approach her with "that lie" again. Thus it is imperative that all members be interviewed alone during a portion of the assessment because the presence of one or more members can greatly influence the disclosures of others.

Once a decision has been made as to which clinicians will conduct the individual interviews, the family is invited into the assessment room and introduced to the clinicians. The family session has three purposes: to observe family communication and interactional patterns, to assess each family member's knowledge of the problems, and to assess the consistency of information when matched with accompanying documents (e.g., police report, CPS petition, medical report, etc.). The family is then separated for the individual interviews.

The parent interview includes the development and social history of the child; medical and psychological information; sexual history; history of marriage, divorce, and/or separation; history of caretakers; and history of physical, sexual, and substance abuse. This is also an opportunity for the clinician to assess the parents' internalization of the reactive behavior and to assess the meaning assigned to the behavior. Families often arrive in crisis because the disclosure may be fairly new, and the clinician may need to provide crisis intervention for several sessions prior to the family's entry into the program. At intake, new disclosures can occur and the parents may need to be informed of a new reporting situation. Debriefing is then required. Anticipatory work around the new abuse report is needed to relieve anxiety and fears and to empower the parent when advocating for the family within the CPS system.

Prior to determining a family's program eligibility, the clinicians gather again to assess information and discuss eligibility. At this point, a more thorough assessment is made with the benefit of information provided by all clinicians. Many times, information is distorted, minimized, rationalized, or left out from the individual interviews. Prior to their departure, the family meets with the clinician team to discuss participation in the program. Other assessment interviews may be required if information is vague, confusing, or if risk issues are unclear.

In order for the family to be included in program, the reactive child must acknowledge and take some ownership of the behavior. (Please refer to Chapter 6, this volume, for specifics.) The parents need to acknowledge the reactive behavior, and all secrets about the abuse must be revealed to all family members. If the reactive child remains in the home with the victim, the family system has to be healthy enough to protect each child and/or there must be a social system supervising the family. Simply put, external controls must be in place so that the reactive child can develop the internal controls to manage his or her behavior. If the parent or reactive child is not appropriate for the group, the parent or child will enter into individual treatment to prepare for entry into the group. Adjunct family and individual services are offered at times of crisis or to work through issues that are not appropriate for the group.

### Parent Group Structure

The group meets once a week for 1½ hours. The last 15 minutes, the parents join the children for social time and a snack. This is a good time for the children's therapists to share the children's progress in group and to observe parent/child interactions.

In the parents' group, the first 5 to 10 minutes are social time when parents get coffee or tea and prepare for the group. At the beginning of each session, the therapists attempt to check in with each member to assess for high-risk and crisis issues, as well as issues of concern. This technique will usually draw out a topic for discussion. The last 10 minutes of group is for winding down, and discussion becomes less intense again so that the parents can prepare for departure.

Both parents and children are involved in parallel learning, which includes structured activity, didactic learning, and family group activities. The focus is on improving communication and interaction regarding sexuality issues. As a benefit, the family develops a safer environment for the reactive child that minimizes the child's chances of reoffending.

## The Parent Conference

Near the end of each cycle, a parent-child conference is scheduled in place of group therapy. At this time, the child's therapist meets with the parents, and their child if the child is willing, in order to discuss progress, concerns, and treatment goals. The children are included to discourage secrets and encourage communication regarding sexuality issues. It is also an opportunity for the clinician to get background information and to assess current family dynamics. The parents' group therapists also are available during this time and they hold an informal group or sit in on conferences to assist parents with processing the information.

Prior to the cycle's end, there is a social gathering to honor the parents and children. The gathering can be the annual Christmas party, a potluck with a multifamily group activity, or a picnic with competitive game play. Parents, children, and therapists participate. It has been our experience that social interactions augment the treatment and healing process. Often, families forget how to play together because they are so consumed with the crisis of the abuse. Families become trusting of the process and each other, and the nature of their group participation becomes more intimate.

## Termination

The family usually stays in treatment from 1 to 1½ years. Termination is evident when the treatment goals have been met and the child has successfully completed the stages of knighthood (for a description, see Chapter 6, this volume). At this point, the child has developed the internal controls to manage his monster and the parents have secured a safe and controlled environment. The support system of personal and professional resources is intact.

The parents and children take part in a knighting ceremony with both parents and children in full costume. The ceremony occurs in a multifamily group at the end of the cycle with the other parents and children in attendance. Certificates and rewards are given to everyone to validate every person's experience. Both parents and children understand that they are welcome to return for services at any time, and they often return for the annual Christmas party, where they give testimony about progress.

> *The family is aware that recovery is a lifelong process.*

The family is aware that recovery is a lifelong process. At any time, life events and/or developmental tasks and issues can trigger unresolved problems or stir new conflicts. Returning for brief treatment is normalized by using the metaphor of physical illness: When we are ill, we go to the doctor, receive treatment, and continue with our daily lives. Later, we might break a leg or have blurred vision, and again we'll seek medical treatment to resolve the malady. It would be unthinkable to put our health in jeopardy by refusing medical services. Parents and children seem amenable to continuing treatment when it is explained to them in this way.

## ■ The Cotherapeutic Team

The cotherapeutic team interacts with group members in a variety of ways. Their roles can be didactic, directive, advocative, therapeutic, and nurturing. Communication styles are relaxed and, at times, humorous. In fact, humor can be quite cathartic: Content issues can be burdening and overwhelming, and humor often alleviates anxiety. The therapists' roles are interchangeable throughout the life of the group depending upon membership need and group process. At times, the therapists can advocate for parents with other systems. It is not uncommon for therapists to meet with other professionals or to attend meetings at children's schools to assist with keeping the school environments safe or developing appropriate education plans.

The cotherapeutic team can sit together or opposite each other as determined by the needs of the group. For example, the team may sit together if the group is splitting to present a united front. In order to observe group member interaction and behavior, the team may sit opposite each other (Yalom, 1985).

Both clinicians are responsible for accepting a variety of roles to model appropriate social, parenting, and interpersonal relationship behaviors. If one team member assumes only the dominant role, the team becomes unbalanced and does not represent a healthy dyad.

## Deviance in Treatment

It is important for the cotherapeutic team to recognize deviancy in treatment. Failure to do so can lead to destruction of the group (Yalom, 1985). According to Yalom (1985), clients deviating significantly from the rest of the group in areas crucial to their participation is the primary reason for premature termination. Deviant behavior specific to this population covers transference, eccentric membership, and sporadic attendance.

One specific transference issue related to this population is that the therapists, especially the children's therapists, are viewed as the good parents, and such thinking increases the parents' feelings of ineffectiveness. Parents have lots of questions about what is occurring in the children's group and why children will disclose abuse details to their therapists but not their parents. The trick is to assist parents in recognizing their own power and ability to parent. Other significant transference behaviors are the group members' sexual transferences, their romanticizing of the therapeutic team, and their views of themselves as critical parents.

Another deviancy in treatment is admitting eccentric members (e.g., a religious extremist who cannot process and work through issues). A young, single parent was admitted to the program, and into each group session she'd tote her briefcase full of Bibles. Unfortunately, she terminated prematurely because she couldn't tolerate the program's content. According to Yalom (1985), clients who deviate significantly from the rest of the group in areas crucial to their participation are the primary reason for premature termination.

Sporadic attendance and missing members can also stymie group progress. Members often fantasize negatively about the absent members and, upon their return, the intimacy level drops tremendously. Self-disclosure, risk-taking behaviors, and trust are at a minimum. It is important to mention absent members at the beginning of each group session and to discuss the extended absences of others throughout the cycle.

> *The belief that "we are only here for our children" prevents parents from mastering treatment goals.*

The belief that "we are only here for our children" prevents parents from mastering treatment goals and limits their participation. Parents who believe this will always remain on the periphery and will never fully enter the group process. These parents are not appropriate for group and should be seen in individual treatment.

Deviancy can also derail a healthy group process. It is the responsibility of the cotherapeutic team to recognize deviant behaviors and to curtail them prior to any damage to group process.

## ■ Treatment Interventions

There is a variety of ways in which the cotherapeutic team can deliver education, support, and interpretation; solidify hope and trust; and bring structure to the group. Techniques such as rituals, storytelling, guest speakers, media, and structured activities accomplish these goals.

### Rituals

At the beginning of each cycle, as new members enter the group, the veteran group members introduce themselves and share how they became involved in the program, who their children are, and how it felt when they were new. This ritual has two benefits: First, it offers the new parents hope and a sense of belonging, and it identifies shared commonalities. Second, the therapist can assess, via members' disclosures, where those members are in recovery. For instance, many parents will identify their children only as victims and will deny the reactive behaviors.

Another ritual used both as new members enter and throughout the group when members are in denial is the reading of *There's No Such Thing As a Dragon* (Kent, 1975). This is a story about a little boy named Billy Bixby who wakes up one morning and notices that there is a tiny dragon in his room. Excited, Billy shares the news with his mother, who retorts, "There's no such thing as a dragon." Billy reluctantly believes his mother and begins to ignore the dragon. However, the dragon grows and grows until it runs away with the house. When Billy finally pays attention to the dragon, it shrinks back to its tiny size. The moral of the story: If you don't pay attention to a problem, it will grow until you can no longer ignore it. This is an excellent beginning ritual because the metaphor is given in a nonthreatening manner and the parents learn that they must face the crisis head on.

## Storytelling and Bibliotherapy

A set of techniques that is also useful is storytelling and/or bibliotherapy. Parents bring in articles, books, and other literature relevant to group content. The "gift" to the group, as well as the reading of the literature, is empowering and healing. Several group sessions can be spent discussing the literature. This is especially useful regarding the issue of parents discussing sex with their children. Talking about ordinary, normal sex is difficult enough, but talking about abnormal sexual experiences is devastating. Reading books with their children opens up lines of communication while creating a safe distance for the parents. According to psychologist Doris Brett, author of *Annie Stories* (1986), storytelling is a way of facing fears or anxieties that are too difficult to verbalize or even identify. Storytelling creates a sense of safety, can be a great release and relief, and models appropriate problem-solving ideas. Billy Bixby's family was an excellent example of facing fears and anxiety.

## Guest Speakers

Guest speakers are another way of imparting information. Members welcome other persons who can validate their experiences. Guests don't necessarily have to be professionals, and laypeople can provide a unique quality that professionals cannot. Laypeople are viewed as more credible because they are seen as peer equals who have, in some way, experienced the same pain and trauma. During one cycle, the group was struggling with understanding victimization issues. A young woman who was molested as a child visited the group and was able to share and communicate in a way that no therapist could.

Another time, the group was struggling with the issue of masturbation. Many group members were actively practicing a form of religion that had strict views on the subject, and only an authority could normalize the reactive behavior. Therefore, a nun who was also a marriage, family, and child counselor provided information about masturbation. Guest speakers on other topics have included sexual health educators and defense attorneys.

## Media

An increasing amount of media attention has been given to the topic of children who molest. Local television programs (e.g., talk shows) and television movies provide excellent content for discussion. Videos can provide information and stimulate discussion of difficult, anxiety-provoking content. The taped show can create a safe distance for group members, who can express feelings and content that otherwise would have been too risky and dangerous to share. Psychodrama and role playing are other ways to get the process going. Parents take on the roles of their children, which lets them experience feelings that otherwise they might not have allowed themselves to experience. Parents can be judgmental and critical, and they can take on a stoic or martyr role in which they withdraw from their children, unable to be the nurturing parents their children need. The psychodrama experience can be quite revealing, and parents appear to internalize their experience, which allows them to master their parental role.

### Structured Activity

One activity that assists parents in dealing with sexuality is quite revealing and, at times, has released repressed memories. Parents and therapists are instructed to write down on a slip of paper their memories of their first sexual experience. The disclosures are put into a box and read aloud anonymously by the therapists. As reflected in the literature, these first experiences are often quite negative. Approximately 85% to 90% of all responses involved coercion, betrayal, and/or a fearful experience. One father who participated in the exercise revealed that his first experience occurred at age 14 when he engaged in a sexual encounter with two adult women. Some time later, after this exercise, he scheduled an individual appointment to discuss memories that resurfaced as a result of the exercise. It was only then that he realized the experience was actually a victimization experience.

After the exercise, parents are led into a discussion of how they perceive their experiences given their religious, cultural, and social influences. Once we have explored their experiences, we discuss sexual messages, and parents ultimately realize what messages they send to their children.

During the human sexuality curriculum (Johnson, 1989b), most of the group sessions are structured with activities. For example, the parents are asked to focus on their own sexual development with attention paid to the cultural, religious, and social influences that shaped their early sexuality and current views of sexuality. They are also encouraged to look at their current sexual identity and the ways they communicate, verbally and nonverbally, to their children regarding sexual matters.

Near the end of the curriculum, multifamily groups are held and families participate in games fashioned after television game shows. For example, "The Newlywed Game," which fosters communication, gives parents and their children a chance to prove what they've learned.

Thus there are a variety of treatment interventions that are instrumental in imparting information to the parents. The nature of the content must be taken into consideration because there may be a need for distancing some group members in order for them to accept the information.

## ■ Summary and Conclusion

The program presented here is clearly for motivated families (even though many are court mandated) and reactive children who are at low risk to reoffend with malice and danger to others. In therapy, the parents must initially restructure their environments to keep their children safe while they battle their own misconceptions and confused feelings. Premature termination often occurs because parents look for a cure and refuse to accept the concept of lifelong management. Those who stay and attend the program must work through personal histories, learn about behaviors related to sex and sexuality, and continue to care for their children.

Via education, support, and therapeutic intervention, the family strengthens itself and reinforces the positive attributes while discarding the negative. Thus parental involvement is essential to the successful treatment and prognosis of the abuse reactive child.

# References

Abel, G. G., Becker, J. V., Mittelman, M., Cunningham-Rathner, J., Rouleau, J. L., & Murphy, W. D. (1987). Self-reported sex crimes of non-incarcerated paraphiliacs. *Journal of Interpersonal Violence, 2,* 3-25.

Achenbach, T. M., & Edelbrock, C. (1983). *Manual for the child behavior checklist and the revised child behavior profile.* Burlington: University of Vermont, Department of Psychiatry.

Anastopoulos, A. D., & Barkley, R. A. (1992). Attention deficit-hyperactivity disorder. In C. E. Walker & M. C. Roberts (Eds.), *Handbook of clinical child psychology* (2nd ed., pp. 413-430). New York: John Wiley.

Beahrs, J. (1991, April). *Strategic self-therapy for disorders of traumatic dissociation.* Paper presented at the Sixth Regional Conference on Multiple Personality and Dissociative States, Akron, OH.

Becker, J. V., & Quinsey, V. L. (1993). Assessing suspected child molesters. *Child Abuse & Neglect, 17,* 169-174.

Beitchman, J. H., Zucker, K. J., Hood, J. E., daCosta, G. A., Akman, D., & Cassavia, E. (1992). A review of the long-term effects of child sexual abuse. *Child Abuse & Neglect, 16,* 101-118.

Berliner, L., & Conte, J. R. (1990). The process of victimization: The victim's perspective. *Child Abuse & Neglect, 14,* 29-40.

Berliner, L., & Conte, J. R. (1993). Sexual abuse evaluations: Conceptual and empirical obstacles. *Child Abuse & Neglect, 17,* 111-126.

Berliner, L., & Wheeler, J. R. (1987). Treating the effects of sexual abuse on children. *Journal of Interpersonal Violence, 2,* 415-434.

Berman, B. D., Winkleby, M., Chesterman, E., & Boyce, W. T. (1992). After school child care and self-esteem in school-age children. *Pediatrics, 89,* 654-659.

Bowlby, J. (1984). Violence in the family as a disorder of the attachment and caregiving systems. *American Journal of Psychoanalysis, 44,* 9-28.

Braswell, L., & Kendall, P. (1985). *Cognitive and behavioral therapy for impulsive children.* New York: Guilford.

Braun, B. G. (1988). The BASK model of dissociation. *Dissociation, 1,* 4-23.

166

Breiner, S. J. (1990). *Slaughter of innocents: Child abuse through the ages and today.* New York: Plenum.

Brett, D. (1986). *Annie stories.* New York: Workman.

Briere, J. (1989a). *Therapy for adults molested as children: Beyond survival.* New York: Springer.

Briere, J. (1989b). *Trauma symptom checklist-children.* Los Angeles: University of Southern California School of Medicine, Department of Psychiatry.

Burgess, A. W., Hartman, C. R., & McCormack, A. (1987). Abused to abuser: Antecedents of socially deviant behaviors. *American Journal of Psychiatry, 144,* 1431-1436.

Camp, B. W., & Bash, M. S. (1975). *Think aloud increasing social and cognitive skills: A problem solving program for children.* Champaign, IL: Research Press.

Cantwell, H. B. (1988). Child sexual abuse: Very young perpetrators. *Child Abuse & Neglect, 12,* 579-582.

Ceci, S. J., Ross, D. T., & Toglia, M. D. (1985). *Suggestibility of children's memory: Psycho-legal implication.* Unpublished abstract, Cornell University, Ithaca, NY.

Children's World. (1993, April). *Child to child sexual behavior in early child care settings.* Paper presented at the 21st Annual Child Abuse and Neglect Symposium, Denver, CO.

Cohen, R. L., & Harnick, M. A. (1980). The susceptibility of child witnesses to suggestion. *Law and Human Behavior, 4,* 201-210.

Cole, P., Woolger, C., Power, T. G., & Smith, K. D. (1992). Parenting difficulties among adult survivors of father-daughter incest. *Child Abuse & Neglect, 16,* 239-250.

Coleman, L. (1989). Issues in child abuse accusations. *Institute for Psychological Therapies, 1,* 1-9.

Committee for Children. (1988). *Second step: A violence prevention curriculum* (Grades 1-3, 4-5, 6-8). Seattle, WA: Author.

Conte, J., & Berliner, L. (1988). The impact of sexual abuse on children: Empirical findings. In L. Walker (Ed.), *Handbook on sexual abuse children* (pp. 72-93). New York: Springer.

Corwin, D. L., & Olafson, E. (1993). Overview: Clinical identification of sexually abused children. *Child Abuse & Neglect, 17,* 3-5.

Cotton, A. (1873). *Woman's work: The Children's Home, Leytonstone.* W. C. Cotton (Ed.). Chester: Philipson and Golden.

Crittenden, P. M., & DiLalla, D. L. (1988). Compulsive compliance: The development of an inhibitory coping strategy in infancy. *Journal of Abnormal Child Psychology, 16,* 585-599.

Deisher, R. W., Wenet, G. A., Paperney, D. M., Clark, T. F., & Fehrenbach, P. A. (1982). Adolescent sexual offense behavior: The role of the physician. *Journal of Adolescent Health Care, 2,* 279-286.

Dempster, H. L., & Roberts, J. (1991). Child sexual abuse research: A methodological quagmire. *Child Abuse & Neglect, 15,* 593-595.

Draucker, C. B. (1989). Cognitive adaptation of female incest survivors. *Journal of Consulting and Clinical Psychology, 57,* 668-670.

Durrell, L. (1978). *Livia or buried alive.* New York: Viking.

Dwyer, K. M., Danley, K. L., Sussman, S. Y., & Johnson, C. A. (1990). Characteristics of eighth-grade students who initiate self-care in elementary and junior high school. *Pediatrics, 86,* 448-454.

Everson, M. D., Hunter, W. M., Runyon, D. K., Edelsohn, G. A., & Coulter, M. L. (1989). Maternal support following disclosure of incest. *American Journal of Orthopsychiatry, 59,* 197-207.

Ewing, C. P. (1990). *When children kill: The dynamics of juvenile homicide.* Lexington, MA: Lexington Books.

Faller, K. C. (1984). Is the child victim of sexual abuse telling the truth? *Child Abuse & Neglect, 8,* 473-481.

Faller, K. C. (1988). Criteria for judging the credibility of children's statements about their sexual abuse. *Child Welfare, 67,* 389-401.

Federal Bureau of Investigation. (1987). *Federal Bureau of Investigation, 2,* 10.

Feldman, W., Feldman, E., Goodman, J. T., McGrath, P. J., Pless, R. P., Corsini, L., & Bennett, S. (1991). Is childhood sexual abuse really increasing in prevalence? An analysis of the evidence. *Pediatrics, 88,* 29-33.

Field, T. (1985). Attachment as psychobiological attunement: Being on the same wave length. In M. Reite & T. Field (Eds.), *The psychobiology of attachment and separation.* Orlando, FL: Academic Press.

Finkelhor, D. (1986). *A sourcebook on child sexual abuse.* Newbury Park, CA: Sage.

Finkelhor, D., & Browne, A. (1985). Initial and long term effects: A conceptual framework. In D. Finkelhohr (Ed.), *Child abuse, new theory and research.* New York: Free Press.

Finkelhor, D., Hotaling, G. T., Lewis, I. A., & Smith, C. (1990). Sexual abuse in a national survey of adult men and women: Prevalence characteristics and risk factors. *Child Abuse & Neglect, 14,* 19-28.

Finkelhor, D., Hotaling, G. T., & Sedlak, A. J. (1992). The abduction of children by strangers and non-family members. *Journal of Interpersonal Violence, 7,* 226-243.

Franklin, B. (1990). Wimps and bullies: Press reporting of child abuse. *Social Work and Social Welfare Yearbook,* pp. 1-14.

Friedrich, W. N. (1988). Behavior problems in sexually abused children: An adaptational perspective. In G. E. Wyatt & G. J. Powell (Eds.), *Lasting effects of child sexual abuse* (pp. 171-191). Newbury Park, CA: Sage.

Friedrich, W. N. (1990). Evaluating the child and planning for treatment. In W. Friedrich (Ed.), *Psychotherapy of sexually abused children and their families* (pp. 64-99). New York: W. W. Norton.

Friedrich, W. N. (1991). Sexual behavior in sexually abused children. In J. Briere (Ed.), *Treating victims of child sexual abuse* (pp. 15-27). San Francisco: Jossey-Bass.

Friedrich, W. N. (1993). Sexual victimization and sexual behavior in children: A review of recent literature. *Child Abuse & Neglect, 17,* 59-66.

Friedrich, W. N., Beilke, R., & Urquiza, A. (1988). Behavior problems in young sexually abused boys. *Journal of Interpersonal Violence, 3,* 21-27.

Friedrich, W. N., Grambsch, P., Broughton, D., Kuiper, J., & Beilke, R. L. (1991). Normative sexual behavior in children. *Pediatrics, 88,* 456-464.

Friedrich, W. N., Grambsch, P., Damon, L., Koverola, C., Hewitt, S., Lang, R., & Wolfe, V. (1992). The child sexual behavior inventory: Normative and clinical comparisons. *Psychological Assessment, 4,* 303-311.

Fromuth, M. E., Burkhart, B. R., & Jones, C. W. (1991). Hidden child molestation. *Journal of Interpersonal Violence, 6,* 376-384.

Gale, J., Thompson, R. J., Moran, T., & Sack, W. H. (1988). Sexual abuse in young children: Its clinical presentation and characteristic patterns. *Child Abuse & Neglect, 12,* 163-170.

Garland, R. J., & Dougher, M. J. (1990). The abused/abuser hypothesis of child sexual abuse: A critical review of theory and research. In J. Feierman (Ed.), *Pedophilia: Biosocial dimensions.* New York: Springer-Verlag.

Gil, E., & Johnson, T. C. (1993). *Sexualized children.* Walnut Creek, CA: Launch Press.

Goodman, G. S., & Helgeson, V. S. (1988). Children as witnesses: What do they remember? In L. E. A. Walker (Ed.), *Handbook on sexual abuse of children.* New York: Springer.

Goodman, G. S., & Jones, D. P. H. (1987, August). *Children's reaction to criminal court testimony.* Paper presented at the annual meeting of the American Psychological Association, New York.

Graziano, A. M., & Namaste, K. A. (1990). Parental use of physical force in child discipline: A survey of 679 college students. *Journal of Interpersonal Violence, 5,* 449-463.

Green, A. H. (1984). Child abuse by siblings. *Child Abuse & Neglect, 8,* 311-317.

Grosz, C. A., Kelly, M., Haase, C., & Kempe, R. (1992, May). *Forum F: Intervention in nonfamilial child sexual abuse: Evaluation and treatment.* Twentieth Annual Child Abuse and Neglect Symposium Conference Syllabus, Keystone, CO.

Groth, N., & Burgess, A. W. (1979). Sexual trauma in the life histories of rapists and child molesters. *Victimology, 4,* 10-16.

Haugaard, J. J., & Tilly, C. (1988). Characteristics predicting children's responses to sexual encounters with other children. *Child Abuse & Neglect, 12,* 209-218.

Henderson, J. E., English, D. J., & MacKenzie, W. R. (1988). Family centered casework practice with sexually aggressive children. In J. S. Wodarski & D. L. Whitaker (Eds.), *Treatment of sex offenders in social work and mental health settings* (pp. 89-108). New York: Haworth.

Hewitt, S. K., & Friedrich, W. N. (1991). Effects of probable sexual abuse on preschool children. In M. Q. Patton (Ed.), *Family sexual abuse: Frontline research and evaluation* (pp. 57-74). Newbury Park, CA: Sage.

Hewlett, S. A. (1991). *When the bough breaks.* New York: HarperCollins.

Hunter, M. (1990). *Abused boys: The neglected victims of sexual abuse.* Lexington, MA: Lexington Books.

Hunter, M., & Gerber, P. (1990). The use of the terms "victim" and "survivor." In M. Hunter (Ed.), *The sexually abused male* (Vol. 2, pp. 79-89). Lexington, MA: Lexington Books.

Isaacs, C. (1992). *Experiences in treating child to child sexual abuse.* Presentation at Summit County, CO. The Redirecting Sexual Aggression Institute, Lakewood, CO.

Jacobvitz, D., & Sroufe, L. A. (1987). The early caregiver-child relationship and attention-deficit disorder with hyperactivity in kindergarten: A prospective study. *Child Development, 58,* 1488-1495.

Johnson, T. C. (1988). Child perpetrators: Children who molest other children: Preliminary findings. *Child Abuse & Neglect, 12,* 219-229.

Johnson, T. C. (1989a). Female child perpetrators: Children who molest other children. *Child Abuse & Neglect, 13,* 571-585.

Johnson, T. C. (1989b). *Human sexuality.* Curriculum for parents and children in troubled families available from Children's Institute International, Marshall Resource Library, Los Angeles, CA.

Johnson, T. C. (1991a). Children who molest children: Identification and treatment approaches for children who molest other children. *The APSAC Advisor, 4*(4), 9-11.

Johnson, T. C. (1991b, August/September). Understanding the sexual behaviors of young children. *SIECUS Report.*

Johnson, T. C., & Berry, C. (1989). Children who molest: A treatment program. *Journal of Interpersonal Violence, 4*, 185-203.

Jones, D., & McQuiston, M. (1987). Reliable and fictitious accounts of sexual abuse to children. *Journal of Interpersonal Violence, 2*, 27-46.

Jones, D. P. H., & Alexander, H. (1987). Treating the abusive family within the family care system. In R. E. Helfer & R. S. Kempe (Eds.), *The battered child* (pp. 339-359). Chicago: University of Chicago Press.

Jones, J. C., & Barlow, D. H. (1990). The etiology of post-traumatic stress disorder. *Clinical Psychology Review, 10*, 299-328.

Kahaner, L. (1988). *Cults that kill: Probing the underworld of occult crime.* New York: Warner.

Kasl, C. D. (1990). Female perpetrators of sexual abuse: A feminist view. In M. Hunter (Ed.), *The sexually abused male* (Vol. 1, pp. 259-274). Lexington, MA: Lexington Books.

Kelly, P. C., Weir, M. R., Atkinson, A. W., Lampe, R. M., Schydlower, M., & Fearnow, R. G. (1986). Latchkey. *Clinical Pediatrics, 25*, 462-465.

Kendall-Tackett, K. A., Williams, L. M., & Finkelhor, D. (1992). The impact of sexual abuse on children: A review and synthesis of recent empirical studies. *Psychological Bulletin, 113*, 164-180.

Kent, J. (1975). *There's no such thing as a dragon.* New York: Western.

Kikuchi, J. J. (1988, Fall). Rhode Island develops successful intervention program for adolescents. *NCASA News,*

Kluft, R. (1989). Editorial: Reflections on allegations of ritual abuse. *Dissociation, 2*(4), 191-193.

Larson, N., & Maddock, W. (1986). Structural and functional variables in incest family systems: Implications for assessment and treatment. In T. Trepper & M. J. Barrett (Eds.), *Treating incest: A multiple systems perspective* (pp. 27-44). New York: Haworth.

Laviola, M. (1992). Effects of older brother-younger sister incest: A study of the dynamics of 7 cases. *Child Abuse & Neglect, 16*, 409-421.

Longo, R. E., & Groth, A. G. (1983). Juvenile sexual offenders in the histories of adult rapists and child molesters. *International Journal of Offender Therapy and Comparative Criminology, 27*, 150-155.

Longo, R. E., & McFadin, B. (1981). Sexually inappropriate behavior: Development of the sexual offender. *Law and Order, 12*, 21-23.

Lorado, C. (1982). Sibling incest. In S. Sgroi (Ed.), *Handbook of clinical interventions in child sexual abuse* (pp. 177-189). Lexington, MA: Lexington Books.

MacFarlane, K., Cockriel, K., & Dugan, M. (1990). Treating victims of incest. In R. K. Oates (Ed.), *Understanding and managing child sexual abuse.* Sydney: Harcourt Brace Jovanovich.

Mandell, J., & Damon, L. (1989). *Group treatment for sexually abused children.* New York: Guilford.

Margolin, L. (1991). Child sexual abuse by non-related care givers. *Child Abuse & Neglect, 15*, 213-221.

Margolin, L., & Craft, J. (1990). Child abuse by adolescent care givers. *Child Abuse & Neglect, 14*, 365-373.

Martinson, F. L. (1991). Normal sexual development in infancy and early childhood. In G. D. Ryan & S. L. Lane (Eds.), *Juvenile sexual offending* (pp. 57-82). Lexington, MA: Lexington Books.

Mathews, R., Mathews, J., & Speltz, K. (1990). Female sexual offenders. In M. Hunter (Ed.), *The sexually abused male* (Vol. 1, pp. 275-294). Lexington, MA: Lexington Books.

McGrath, R. J. (1990). Assessment of sexual aggressors. *Journal of Interpersonal Violence, 5,* 507-519.

McLeer, S., Deblinger, E., Atkins, M., Foa, E., & Ralphe, D. (1988). Post-traumatic stress disorder in sexually abused children. *Journal of the American Academy of Child and Adolescent Psychiatry, 27,* 650-654.

Medved, M. (1992). *Hollywood vs. America.* New York: HarperCollins.

Miau, M. (1986). Review of 125 children 6 years of age and under who were sexually abused. *Child Abuse & Neglect, 10,* 223-229.

Miller, B. C., Christopherson, C. R., & King, P. K. (1993). Sexual behavior in adolescence. In T. P. Gullotta, G. R. Adams, & R. Montemayor (Eds.), *Adolescent sexuality* (pp. 57-76). Newbury Park, CA: Sage.

Moll, A. (1913). *Sexual life of the child* (E. Paul, Trans.). New York: Macmillan.

Morgan, R. F. (1990, April). *Behavioral problems of children likely to parallel sleep difficulties.* Paper presented at the Southeastern Psychological Association Conference, Atlanta, GA.

Morris, R. J., & Kratochwill, T. R. (1983). *Treating children's fears and phobias.* New York: Pergamon.

Mulhern, S. (1990). Incest: A laughing matter. *Child Abuse & Neglect, 14*(2), 265-271.

Mussen, P. (1975). Communication and the development of prosocial behavior. *American Speech and Hearing Association, 17,* 324-330.

Olafson, E., Corwin, D. L., & Summit, R. C. (1993). Modern history of child sexual abuse awareness: Cycles of discovery and suppression. *Child Abuse & Neglect, 17,* 7-24.

Patterson, G., Reid, J. B., Jones, R. R., & Conger, R. E. (1975). *A social learning approach to family intervention: Vol. 1: Families with aggressive children.* Eugene, OR: Castalia.

Perry, B. D. (1993a). Neurodevelopment and the neurophysiology of trauma: I. Conceptual considerations for clinical work with maltreated children. *APSAC Advisor, 6*(1), 1, 14-18.

Perry, B. D. (1993b). Neurodevelopment and the neurophysiology of trauma: II. Conceptual considerations for clinical work with maltreated children. *APSAC Advisor, 6*(2), 1, 14-20.

Porter, E. (1986). *Treating the young male victim of sexual assault: Issues and intervention strategies.* Orwell, VT: Safer Society Press.

Reinhart, M. A. (1987). Sexually abused boys. *Child Abuse & Neglect, 11,* 229-235.

Richardson, J., Best, J., & Bromley, D. (1991). *The satanism scare.* New York: de Gruyter.

Richardson, J. L., McGuigan, K., Johnson, C. A., & Brannon, B. (1989). Substance use among eighth-grade students who take care of themselves after school. *Pediatrics, 84,* 556-566.

Rissin, L., & Koss, M. (1987). Prevalence and descriptive characteristics of childhood victimizations. *Journal of Interpersonal Violence, 2,* 309-323.

Ryan, G. (1987). Juvenile sex offenders: Development and correction. *Child Abuse & Neglect, 11,* 385-395.

Ryan, G. (1991a). Juvenile sex offenders: Defining the population. In G. D. Ryan & S. L. Lane (Eds.), *Juvenile sexual offending* (pp. 3-8). Lexington, MA: Lexington Books.

Ryan, G. (1991b). Incidence and prevalence of sexual offenses committed by juveniles. In G. D. Ryan & S. L. Lane (Eds.), *Juvenile sexual offending* (pp. 9-16). Lexington, MA: Lexington Books.

Ryan, G., Blum, J., Law, S., Astler, L., Sandau-Christopher, D., Sundine, C., Dale, J., & Teske, J. (1989). *Understanding and responding to the sexual behavior of children: Trainer's manual.* Denver: Kempe Center.

Ryan, G., Lane, S., Davis, J., & Isaac, C. (1987). Juvenile sex offenders: Development and correction. *Child Abuse & Neglect, 11,* 385-395.

Ryder, D. (1992). *Breaking the circle of satanic ritual abuse: Recognizing and recovering from the hidden trauma.* Minneapolis, MN: CompCare.

Sakheim, D., & Devine, S. (1992). *Out of darkness: Exploring satanism and ritual abuse.* New York: Lexington Books.

Sanders, D. G. (1991). Procedures for adjusting self reports of violence for social desirability bias. *Journal of Interpersonal Violence, 6,* 336-344.

Santostefano, S. (1986). Cognitive controls, metaphors, and context: An approach to cognition and emotion. In D. Bearson & H. Zimilies (Eds.), *Thoughts and emotion* (pp. 175-210). Hillsdale, NJ: Lawrence Erlbaum.

Scott, W. (1992). Group therapy with sexually abused boys: Notes toward managing behavior. *Clinical Social Work Journal, 20,* 395-409.

Selman, R. L., & Schultz, L. H. (1990). *Making a friend in youth: Developmental theory in pair therapy.* Chicago: University of Chicago Press.

Sgroi, S. M. (1982). *Handbook of clinical intervention in child sexual abuse.* Lexington, MA: Lexington Books.

Sgroi, S. M., Bunk, B. S., & Wabrek, C. J. (1988). Children's sexual behaviors and their relationship to sexual abuse. In S. Sgroi (Ed.), *Vulnerable populations: Evaluation and treatment of sexually abused children and adult survivors* (Vol. 1, pp. 1-24). Lexington, MA: Lexington Books.

Siever, L. J., & Davis, K. L. (1985). Overview: Toward a dysregulation hypothesis of depression. *American Journal of Psychiatry, 142,* 1017-1031.

Simkins, L. (1991). Characteristics of sexually repressed child molesters. *Journal of Interpersonal Violence, 8,* 3-17.

Simon, L. M. J., Salas, B., Kazniak, A., & Kahn, M. (1992). Characteristics of child molesters. *Journal of Interpersonal Violence, 7,* 211-225.

Simpson, A. E. (1988). Vulnerability and the age of female consent: Legal innovation and its effect on prosecutions for rape in eighteenth century London. In G. S. Rousseau & R. Porter (Eds.), *Sexual underworlds of the Enlightenment* (pp. 181-205). Chapel Hill: University of North Carolina Press.

Smets, A., & Cebula, C. M. (1987). A group treatment program for adolescent sex offenders: 5 steps toward resolution. *Child Abuse & Neglect, 11,* 247-254.

Smith, M., & Pazder, L. (1981). *Michele remembers.* New York: Congdon & Lattes.

Smolensky, S., & Goodman, G. S. (1987). *Distinguishing the pretend from the real: Even young children can do it.* Unpublished manuscript.

Spivack, G., & Shure, M. B. (1974). *Social adjustment of young children: A cognitive approach to solving real-life problems.* San Francisco: Jossey-Bass.

Steele, B. (1987). Reflections on the therapy of those who maltreat children. In R. E. Helfer & R. S. Kempe (Eds.), *The battered child* (pp. 382-391). Chicago: University of Chicago Press.

Stein, A., & Lewis, D. O. (1992). Discovering physical abuse: Insights from a follow-up study of delinquents. *Child Abuse & Neglect, 16,* 523-531.

Steinglass, P., Bennett, L. A., Wolin, S. J., & Reiss, D. (1987). *The alcoholic family.* New York: Basic Books.

Strean, H., & Freeman, L. (1991). *Our wish to kill: The murder in all our hearts.* New York: St. Martin's.

Stroh, G. (1991a, April). *Ritual abuse: Confronting the beast within*. Paper presented at the Sixth Regional Conference for the Study of Multiple Personality and Dissociative States, Akron, OH.

Stroh, G. (1991b, November). *Abreact ≠ re-enact*. Paper presented at the Eighth International Conference for the Study of Multiple Personality and Dissociative States, Chicago.

Stroh, G. (1992, April). *The therapeutic use of boundaries and limit setting with individuals diagnosed with a dissociative disorder*. Symposium at the Seventh Regional Conference for the Study of Multiple Personality and Dissociative States, Akron, OH.

Stroh, G. (1993, May). *Ritual abuse: Fact or fiction?* Symposium at Michigan State University.

Summit, R. C. (1988). Hidden victims, hidden pain: Society's avoidance of child sexual abuse. In G. E. Wyatt & G. J. Powell (Eds.), *Lasting effects of child sexual abuse* (pp. 39-60). Newbury Park: Sage.

Tardieu, A. A. (1873). *Etude medicale-legale sur les attentats aux moeurs* (6th ed.). Paris.

Taylor, S. E. (1983). Adjustment to threatening events: A theory of cognitive adaptation. *American Psychologist, 38*, 1161-1173.

Terr, L. (1981). Forbidden games: Post-traumatic child's play. *American Journal of Orthopsychiatry, 20*, 740-759.

Thoennes, N., & Tjaden, P. G. (1990). The extent, nature and validity of sexual abuse allegations in custody/visitation disputes. *Child Abuse & Neglect, 14*, 151-163.

Urquiza, A. J., & Capra, M. (1990). The impact of sexual abuse: Initial and long-term effects. In M. Hunter (Ed.), *The sexually abused male* (Vol. 1, pp. 105-135). Lexington, MA: Lexington Books.

Urquiza, A. J., & Keating, L. M. (1990). The prevalence of sexual victimization of males. In M. Hunter (Ed.), *The sexually abused male* (Vol. 1, pp. 89-103). Lexington, MA: Lexington Books.

Van Benschoten, S. (1990). Multiple personality disorder and satanic ritual abuse: The issue of credibility. *Dissociation, 3*(1), 22-30.

van der Kolk, B. A. (1988). The biological response to psychic trauma. In F. M. Ochberg (Ed.), *Post-traumatic therapy and victims of violence* (pp. 25-39). New York: Brunner/Mazel.

Vander Mey, B., & Neff, R. (1982). Adult-child incest: A review of research and treatment. *Adolescence, 17*, 717-735.

Waterman, J. (1986). Effects of sexual abuse on children. In K. MacFarlane & J. Waterman (Eds.), *Sexual abuse of young children* (pp. 101-118). New York: Guilford.

Watkins, B., & Bentovim, A. (1992). Male children and adolescents as victims: A review of current knowledge. In G. C. Mezey & M. B. King (Eds.), *Male victims of sexual assault* (pp. 27-66). New York: Oxford University Press.

Wedge, T. (1988). *The Satan hunter*. Canton, OH: Daring Books.

Weinberg, S. K. (1955). *Incest behavior*. New York: Citadel.

Werner, H. (1948). *Comparative psychology of mental development*. New York: International Universities Press.

Yalom, I. D. (1985). *The theory & practice of group psychotherapy*. New York: Basic Books.

Zimbardo, P. G., LaBerge, S., & Butler, L. D. (1993). Psychophysiological consequence of unexplained arousal: A post-hypnotic suggestion paradigm. *Journal of Abnormal Psychology, 102*, 466-473.

Zylke, J. W. (1988). Among latchkey children problems: Insufficient day-care facilities, data on possible harm. *Journal of the American Medical Association, 260*, 3399-3400.

# Index

# *About the Editor*

**Mic Hunter** is a Licensed Psychologist, Licensed Marriage & Family Therapist, Certified Chemical Dependency Counselor—Reciprocal, and a Nationally Certified Alcohol and Drug Counselor. His educational background includes a bachelor's degree in psychology (Macalester College), a Master of Arts degree in human development (Saint Mary's College, Winona), and a Master of Science degree in education/psychological services (University of Wisconsin—Superior). He has completed the Alcohol/Drug Counseling Education Program (University of Minnesota), the Two Year Intensive Post-Graduate Program (the Gestalt Institute of the Twin Cities), and the Chemical Dependency and Family Intimacy Training Project (University of Minnesota). He is currently studying for a doctoral degree in clinical psychology (Minnesota School of Professional Psychology). He completed his class work in 1994.

Prior to opening his practice in St. Paul, Minnesota, he was employed in several chemical dependency treatment programs and mental health centers in Minnesota. He speaks throughout the country to both professional audiences and the general public. He has presented at the annual meetings of the American Association of Sex Educators, Counselors & Therapists; the Society for the Scientific Study of Sex; and the American Orthopsychiatric Association. He has presented at all five national conferences on male sexual abuse survivors and has given a keynote address at the conference in Tucson. He has been interviewed by the print and broadcast media more than 100 times. He serves on the editorial board of the *Journal of Child Sexual Abuse, Journal of Men's Studies,* and *Moving Forward.*

In addition to articles and chapters, Mr. Hunter is the author of *Abused Boys: The Neglected Victims of Sexual Abuse, The First Step for People in Relationships With Sex Addicts, Joyous Sexuality: Healing From Family Sexual Dysfunction, The Twelve Steps & Shame,* and *Recovering From Shame Through the Twelve Steps.* He is the contributing editor of *The Sexually Abused Male: Volume 1. Prevalence, Impact and Treatment* and *The Sexually Abused Male: Volume 2. Application of Treatment Strategies,* as well as *Adult Survivors of Sexual Abuse: Treatment Innovations* (Sage, 1995). His most recent projects are coauthoring *The Use of Touch in Psychotherapy* with Peter Dimock and Jim Struve, which will be submitted for publication in early 1995, and seeking a publisher for his photographic documentary focusing on the disappearance of the traditional male barbershop, which is titled *The Barbershop: An American Classic.*

# *About the Contributors*

**Sandra Ballester,** PsyD, has worked in the field of abuse and neglect for more than 10 years, with extensive experience in the treatment of sexual abuse, in diagnostic assessment, and in working with the court system. She was the supervising psychologist in the Child Abuse Treatment and Support Program (CATS) and the Support Program for Abuse Reactive Kids (SPARK) at Children's Institute International, a nonprofit agency developed to respond to the needs of families and victims of child abuse. Prior to this, she coordinated a sexual abuse group treatment program that served more than 100 clients and also coordinated a court education program (KICS) for child witnesses. In 1990, she participated in a research study on the sexually abused population served at Harbor-UCLA Medical Center. Dr. Ballester, along with her colleague, Frederique Pierre, are internationally recognized for their work with abuse reactive children. Their work has been highlighted in articles in *Rolling Stone* and *Newsweek* magazines.

**Armond Boldi** has been involved in the field of child abuse for the past 12 years as a marriage, family, and child counselor. He has worked with victims as well as perpetrators. He has served as a part-time faculty member at the California State University in Los Angeles, where he lectured to students on family studies and child abuse and neglect. Currently, Mr. Boldi maintains a private practice in Montebello, California, and is the Director for the Family Care Center at Children's

Institute International in Torrance, California. He has traveled extensively, providing training to organizations throughout the country.

**Sally Cantor,** LCSW, BCD, is a 1973 graduate of the Columbia University School of Social Work. Since 1987, she has been involved in developing inpatient treatment programs for adolescent and child survivors of sexual abuse. She is currently Director of Sexual Abuse Therapy at MeadowWood Hospital in New Castle, Delaware, and Director of Sexual Abuse Therapy for Child and Adolescent Services at Northwestern Institute in Fort Washington, Pennsylvania. Ms. Cantor has been recognized as an expert witness regarding child sexual abuse in the criminal courts of Delaware. She serves as a consultant and trainer to child protective agencies throughout the country.

**Hendrika B. Cantwell,** MD, is currently a Clinical Professor of Pediatrics at the University of Colorado Health Sciences Center and Consultant on Child Abuse and Neglect for the Colorado Department of Social Services. Her BA was awarded by Barnard College and her MD was earned at the University of Rochester Medical School. Since 1975, she has served as the pediatric consultant for the City of Denver's Child Protection Agency and taken part in 30,000 cases. In addition to numerous articles, she is the coauthor of *Child Neglect.* For her work, she has been the recipient of the Brandt F. Steele and the C. Henry Kempe awards and has been named to the Colorado Women's Hall of Fame. In her spare time, she enjoys skiing and hiking with her husband, William, and her three children (who now have to wait for their parents). Babysitting her three grandsons is her newest pleasure.

**William N. Friedrich,** PhD, is Professor and Consultant to the Division of Psychology in the Department of Psychiatry and Psychology at the Mayo Clinic in Rochester, Minnesota. He is a Diplomate of the American Board of Professional Psychology in both Clinical Psychology and Family Psychology. In addition to numerous research articles, he is the author of *Casebook of Sexual Abuse Treatment* and *Psychotherapy of Sexually Abused Children and Their Families.*

**Diane R. Griggs,** LCSW, has worked in the field of child abuse and neglect for more than 12 years. She has worked with adult and child victims and perpetrators, as well as their families. She was the co-coordinator for the Support Program for Abuse Reactive Kids (SPARK) at Children's Institute International in Los Angeles, where she had been running the parents' group since 1985. She has consulted and provided training to organizations throughout the country, and her work has been highlighted in local media and in the *American Medical Association News*. She also maintains a private practice in Inglewood, California, and is a part-time professor at the Department of Social Welfare at the University of California at Los Angeles.

**Jacqueline Jackson Kikuchi,** MS, is the Coordinator of Education and Prevention Programs at the Rhode Island Rape Crisis Center. For 7 years, she has developed and presented awareness and prevention programs on all areas of sexual abuse, assault, and harassment for children, adolescents, adults, and professionals. She is also pursuing a doctorate in psychology at the University of Rhode Island.

**Frederique Pierre,** LCSW, has worked in the field of child abuse for more than 12 years. She has worked with children and adolescents in a variety of settings, including schools, hospitals, and residential programs. She was the co-coordinator for the Support Program for Abuse Reactive Kids (SPARK) at Children's Institute International in Los Angeles. She and her colleague, Sandra Ballester, are internationally recognized for their work with abuse reactive children. Their work has been highlighted in articles in *Rolling Stone* and *Newsweek* magazines.

**Gayle M. Stroh,** MA, LLP, has a private practice in Okemos, Michigan, and is the program coordinator/consulting psychologist for a partial hospitalization program in Grand Blanc, Michigan, that treats individuals who have experienced severe trauma in childhood. Many of these patients use dissociation as a primary defense style. The program has been in existence since 1986 and has treated more than 200 patients. She has presented papers at the International Conference for Multiple Personality and Dissociation on numerous occasions. While working on her dissertation at Michigan State University, she also finds time to facilitate workshops and seminars throughout the country.